The Fruit Wars

Devotionals for your daily life

by Jeanette Duby
Speaker and Author

THE FRUIT WARS

THE FRUIT

WARS

Devotional Book

by Jeanette Duby

Speaker and Author

The Fruit Wars

Cover Design: Bethany Mayhew & Nicole Hackart
Interior Design: Bethany Mayhew & Nicole Hackart
Photo on back cover – Debi Smith Photography

Library of Congress – Copyright 1-813204710

Duby, Jeanette2012
        The Fruit Wars
Summary: Devotionals for those who like a little inspiration in their daily lives.

Includes bibliographical references.

Printed in the United States of America

Basis for "The Fruit Wars"

"The Fruit Wars" is a compilation of devotionals based on Jesus' teaching in John 15:5 which says, "I am the vine; you are the branches. If a man remains in me and I in him, he will bear much fruit; apart from me you can do nothing."

In today's world, it is difficult to bear fruit. The world does not always lend itself to growing closer to Jesus Christ.

Every day, we face new temptations and challenges that make it difficult to live for Jesus.

"The Fruit Wars" comes out of the struggles we face everyday getting the Word out, the battles we go through to *bear fruit*.

Join me for inspirational, lighthearted, devotionals featuring some real life experiences, humor, and God's Word.

I am not a fancy writer, and sometimes my grammar is incorrect, but the purpose remains the same. I am here to share God's Word with you. I am here to bear fruit - fruit that will last.

So sit back, grab your favorite cup of joe, and enjoy *The Fruit Wars*!

Table of Contents

Dedicated to the One I Love

I would like to dedicate this book to my wonderful daughter, Nicole.

When I think of the many blessings in my life, she has been the greatest. For such a young woman, she is one of the most mature, young women I know. She has a heart for God. I love it when she posts scripture on Facebook. I love the way she asks her friends for their prayer requests. I love the woman she is becoming. My prayer for her is that God would continue to lead her, and she would continue to follow.

My sweetie, you have enormous potential to change the world we live in. You have what it takes, and as your mom, I could not be more proud of you. What a blessing you have been in my life. I know God has been watching over me, because He gave you to me.

Thank you for helping me write this book.

Thank you for your inspiration and support.

Thank you for helping me with the templates and teaching me how to navigate around the computer.

Please continue to pray that this little book brings people closer to God. Together, we can bring glory to God.

Love you,

Mom

Foreword

Often, when we start hearing that the call of Jesus is to live our life completely and confidently for Him, we will nod in agreement and enthusiasm. But as we are bobbing our heads up and down we are silently cutting our eyes to those around us to see if anyone has a look of panic on their face. We are looking for a hint of questioning, doubt, or confusion because, well...to be honest...it is the same feeling we are struggling with. We know we are supposed to follow Jesus, but the ragged truth for many people is we don't know what that is supposed to look like!

The call that Jesus offers to each one of us is the same that He extended to his first disciples. It is simple yet profound, "Follow me..."

So we try to start following and it slowly dawns on us that instead of giving us a clear view of the interstate, He gives us a clear view of the next stepping stone. After we are firmly planted on it, then and only then do we get a view of the next...and so it goes.

Step by step, day in and day out, sometimes we sense that we really have it all together and then other days we feel like we are just wandering aimlessly.

Inside, we think to ourselves, why can't this be easier? It seems like I am always following Jesus and He keeps taking me to surprising places and showing me surprising things. Eventually we discover that when Jesus said,

"Follow me..." He wasn't kidding and He really does intend for us to move.

The Fruit Wars is a devotion book that will get you moving. Each turn of the page will give you another stepping stone in the journey that God has called you to. Whether you find yourself standing at the door of Dwight Howard's home or even pondering what it would be like to ride a bicycle with no pedals, you will be reminded that the path that Jesus has called us to travel is nothing short of the adventure of a lifetime.

As I teach, I tell people, "The unknown with God is better than the known without Him."

Jeanette takes us out of our comfort zone and into this amazing journey into the unknown with joy, excitement, and enthusiasm. I know you will be blessed and better for taking it.

So get started... *The Fruit Wars* are about to begin...start turning the pages!

Jeff Dixon
Transformational Architect
Author of *"The Key to the Kingdom"* and *"Unlocking the Kingdom"*

A Bit about the Author

I am glad you are here. Allow me to share a little history with you.

In 1999, I moved to the Orlando area. Little did I know, God had been working in my life as far back as I could recall.

A dear friend invited me to her church. It was a little Baptist church. It was there I fell in love with preaching. Something touched my heart that day, and my life has never been the same.

I graduated from Baptist College of Florida with an AA degree in Divinity at the age of forty-five. During the last several years, I have experienced many wonderful things. I feel like God and I are riding in the front seat of the car, driving here and there, on a mission. I have seen God do so many spectacular things, and answer so many prayers.

I finally figured out after all these years; Jesus is where joy and happiness are located. Those two things my friend, are more valuable than precious silver, more weighty than gold.

Some day when I am standing before the throne and Jesus is standing there looking at me, I hope to hear Him say, "Well done, good and faithful servant."

Introduction

My desire to write came at a very early age. It started in the fourth grade. Over the years my writing has taken various twists and turns with hit-and-miss jaunts of scratched ideas, outdated software, and several attempts to successfully find a home for my work.

What I realized in those failed endeavors was two things - I was striving to write the wrong things and seeking the wrong home for my work.

God had a better plan in mind. It began to show itself in early 2012 in the form of a simple devotional email to a few friends. What started out as a quick communication of God's Word among friends, quickly spawned into something I would not have imagined – my own website, a texting campaign, and two devotional books.

I think it's safe to say I finally found my rightful place in writing. I finally found the right home.

I am delighted to share this with you. What I'm sharing with you in the pages to come is a wonderful gift from God. It combines memories recalled as well as the wonderful blessing of my new life lived for Christ.

Folks, I had no idea what would happen to me in 1999 when I moved to Central Florida. I didn't know what to do with it or how to respond. I have figured it out, and I would like to encourage you to answer the call, and follow. Don't be afraid of where the road will lead, but instead be obedient to the Father. Trust me when I say, "It's sweeter than the best berry on the vine."

I owe all I have to my Heavenly Father and to Him all praise be given!

Fruit Wars

When I was a kid, my brothers and I used to have fruit wars in the alley behind our house. We would get our friends, several metal garbage cans with lids, tons of fruit from the neighbor trees, ripe and rotten, and set up battle stations. The lids were our shields, the cans our forts. Then with very little skill, a hard throw, and good aim, we would nail each other with fruit. Depending on the condition of the lime or orange, and your throw, you could inflict great pain in the other person, especially if you hit them square in the back and made juice. The key to victory was knocking down their makeshift garbage can fort, thus blasting them with rotten fruit.

What was the key to winning or losing the fruit war? It was the condition of the fruit. A newly ripe orange or lime flies at greater speed than a rotten one. If you do not believe me, go outside and test it for yourself.

I am reminded about the fruit we are to bear. Is it ripe and beneficial for all to eat, or has our fruit shriveled up?

Are we bearing fruit as Jesus commanded? He said in John 15:16: "You did not choose me, but I chose you and appointed you to go and bear fruit - fruit that will last. Then my Father will give you whatever you ask in my name."

Are we doing what Jesus commanded? Are we bearing fruit that will last? Perhaps you are still tending to your vines, still watching, and waiting for the fruit to appear.

Maybe you are like I used to be, I did not know how to bear fruit.

Prayer Time

Father, I thank you for sending your son, Jesus for me. Lord, I thank you for His lesson on bearing fruit. Father, not everyone understands what it looks like to bear fruit. Some are still waiting for their vines to produce fruit. It is a process we go through, and like fruit trees, we all started with a seed. You or someone planted the seeds in us to grow, one day to bear fruit - fruit that will last.

We thank you Lord, for you are the gardener who tends to us, and provides everything we need to grow, and one day to produce fruit that makes a difference in this world. In your son's name, I pray all those things, Amen.

Fruit Wars – The Sequel

I am already laughing at the title of this one because when I think of sequels, they usually are not as good as the original movie. I know there have been a few exceptions, but still. Back to the fruit wars shall we:

The fruit brings to mind something important for us to remember. All fruit comes from a seed. The seed is planted or dropped to the ground, sprouts, grows into a beautiful tree, and in the season, produces fruit. Maybe you have an orange tree in your yard. Perhaps you have a lemon tree. By the way, lemons hurt worse when hit with one because of their shape. I am not trying to say I know from experience - well, maybe a tad bit.

My point is the fruit did not just appear. It went through a process. It started as a seed and made the long journey out to the end of the branch. Through the journey, it experienced many seasons. It went through the hot summers and it battled the freezing temperatures. It became home for many of God's animals like birds, squirrels, and butterflies. In many cases it endured pruning. Pruning fruit trees help promote growth.

Look at what Jesus said in John 15:1-2:

"I am the true vine and my Father is the gardener. He takes away every branch that does not bear fruit in me. He prunes every branch that bears fruit so that it will bear more fruit. "

My footnote says," the grapevine was a symbol of a single vine that supports many branches and bears many grapes."

Christ is the vine, and God is the gardener who cares for the branches to make them fruitful. The branches are all those who claim to be followers of Christ. I will talk about the difference between fruitful branches and non-bearing branches in the next devotional.

Prayer Time

Father, thank you for being the gardener in our life. I pray Lord we allow the pruning to take place in us. I pray we are all trying to bear fruit, fruit that will last. Help everyone to have a blessed day. God, to you be all the glory for these daily devotionals. In Christ Jesus I pray, Amen.

To Fruit or not to Fruit – That is the Question

I just crack myself up with these titles. I might be the only one who thinks they are funny, but it wakes me up in the morning. I am a goober. I cannot help it.

I promised I would talk about the difference between fruit bearing and non-fruit bearing. What does that mean anyway? How does one go about producing fruit? Is pruning painful? Due to the length of the lesson, this will span over several pages. You will be getting it in small portions, or should I say, "*pieces of fruit*"?

Let's go back to John 15:1-3:

"I am the true vine and my Father is the gardener. He takes away every branch that does not bear fruit in me. He prunes every branch that bears fruit so that it will bear more fruit. You are clean already because of the word that I have spoken to you."

I mentioned that fruitful branches are true believers in Christ. You can tell by their daily living and union with Christ. They produce much fruit. However, there are those who are unproductive, they do not produce fruit. Those are the ones who have turned back from following Christ. They made a superficial commitment to Him, and in doing so, they will be separated from the vine. Who is the vine? Jesus. Who are the branches? We are. What are we supposed to do? Produce fruit.

It would be like the seed planted, took root, started to grow, but its branches turned, coiled, and retreated from fully sprouting to the point of extending and producing the little fruit on the end. Like an unproductive fruit tree, unproductive followers are of no use, and will be cut off and tossed aside.

Maybe someone in your life is saying they do not want to be a fruit tree. They want to be a palm tree, or worse yet a weed. Maybe you are asking yourself if you are a fruit tree. We will talk more about the branches in the next few pages. Do not go anywhere.

Prayer Time

Lord, I thank you for your time today and for the message you shared with me. I thank you Lord for taking something as simple as a fruit tree, and using it to get the point across in our lives. It gives us something we are all familiar.

Father, if there is someone in our life who has turned back from you, not wanting to blossom and produce, or even seek you right now, Lord we pray for them. We stand in the gap for them, and ask you to water them, to be a gardener to them, so they may turn to you.

Father, we ask for forgiveness of our sins, and to cleanse us a new. In your son's name, I pray all these things, Amen.

The Branches

Hello. Hope everything is going well. As I mentioned previous, I am going to talk about the branches.

The branches are an important part of the tree. Without them extending out, giving the fruit a place to grow and hang from, we would not have a very good fruit tree. Let's look at John 15:1-4:

"I am the true vine and my Father is the gardener. He takes away every branch that does not bear fruit in me. He prunes every branch that bears fruit so that it will bear more fruit. You are clean already because of the word that I have spoken to you. Remain in me, and I will remain in you. Just as the branch cannot bear fruit by itself, unless it remains in the vine, so neither can you unless you remain in me."

Let's break this down for a second.

Jesus is making a distinction here between two kinds of pruning. In the first part of verse two, He says, "he takes away every branch that does not bear fruit in me." It would be similar to me trimming a tree in the yard that has not produced anything, or it may even be dead.

Next, He says, "he prunes every branch that bears fruit." It would be the same or similar to me pruning a tree in my yard, cutting it back so it blossoms more. If you know anything about trimming bushes or trees, you know what I am referring to. We trim the trees to promote growth. We go through that as people too.

Sometimes God must discipline us (prune us) to strengthen our character and faith. But those that do not bear fruit are cut off from the trunk, because not only are they worthless, but they often infect the rest of the tree. People, who will not bear fruit for God or who try to block the efforts of Gods followers, will be cut off from Gods life giving power.

Jesus says in verse four, "Remain in me and I will remain in you." When we think about the fruit tree, a branch cannot bear fruit unless it stays attached to the vine.

Remember earlier I said a tree starts as a little seed and grows into a tree, having gone through the whole process from start to finish. The branch will die if it does not stay attached. If the branch does not stay attached, there will be no fruit. If the branch is dead or dying, there will be no fruit. Therefore, we as branches, in order to produce fruit, must stay attached to the vine. That vine is Jesus Christ.

Today, who is your branch attached to, and is it alive, dying, or already dead? Are you currently going through the pruning process? Are you being discarded or being disciplined?

Prayer Time

Lord, I pray today for myself and the person reading this right now. The pruning process can be painful, but I know from experience, it is required if we are to produce more fruit. Just like my orange tree in the back yard, if I do not care for it, it will die. Lord, I am thankful you are my gardener, because when I look at my orange tree in the back yard, obviously, I am a terrible gardener. Father, give us the courage today to ask you who our branch is attached to and what process we are in. If we find Lord, we are dying or almost dead, please help us to come back to life, to come back to the vine. In your son's name, I pray all these things, Amen.

Useful or Firewood?

Previously we talked about pruning. Pruning is never a fun thing to go through. It can be painful at times.

It reminded me of when I was ten, and I did not want to comb my long, red hair every day. My mother decided she would fix that problem. She had it cut very short and gave it a tight perm. My long, beautiful, red hair - GONE! She pruned it all right. Do not ask me how that memory has anything to do with fruit. Considering the author, you might make a connection. And no, I did not think it was cute. This is my memory, remember?

Anyway, let's look at John 15 again. Yes, we are still in John 15 for those who are keeping track.

John 15:5-6: "I am the vine, you are the branches. If man remains in me and I in him, he will bear much fruit. Apart from me, you can do nothing. If anyone does not remain in me, he is like a branch that is thrown away and such branches are picked up, thrown into the fire, and burned."

Yikes! Talk about painful. I could become tinder?? What does this mean exactly? How do I remain in Christ?

My footnote says there are five basic ways to remain in Christ.

1. Believe that He is God's son. Read 1 John 4:15.

2. Receive Him as Savior and Lord. Read John 1:12.

3. Do what God says. Read 1 John 3:24.

4. Continue to believe the Gospel. Read 1 John 2:24.

5. Relate in love to the community of believers, Christ's body. Read John 15:12.

Prayer Time

Lord, I am so thankful that my branches are attached to the Vine. They are attached to you, and drawing life from you Lord every day. Lord, may I continue to stay attached to you, and help me to bear fruit.

If anyone reading this today feels like they may be a branch that has been cut off from the vine and tossed aside, I pray they would find their way back to you, start over with a new branch, one connected to you to bear fruit, fruit that will last. Thank you for sending your son to die on the cross for me and my friends. In His name I pray, Amen.

Does this Ever End?

Let's get back to the branches (us).

John 15: 5-6: "I am the vine, you are the branches. If man remains in me and I in him, he will bear much fruit. Apart from me, you can do nothing. If anyone does not remain in me, he is like a branch that is thrown away and such branches are picked up, thrown into the fire, and burned."

We know many people who attempt to be good, honest, and try to do what is right. We also try to do what is good and honest. But Jesus says that the only way to live a truly good life is to stay close to Him. Do not shoot the messenger here.

How do we stay close to Him? Like a branch which stays close to the vine, we are to stay close to Him. In the previous devotional, I outlined five ways to do that.

Therefore, if I am a branch, and I do not stay close to the vine (Jesus), the things I do are not going to be very fruitful, if at all, and Christ will not be a part of them. My efforts will be unfruitful, no lemons, oranges or limes from me. *"NO FRUIT FOR YOU!"*

Every tree that grows needs nourishment, right? We do too. Our branches need nourishment if we are to produce fruit. Our branches need Christ. He gives us what we need every day to grow stronger and more productive. Fruit trees become useless if they are not nourished. You can look at the orange tree in my back yard and see that. It is struggling.

The question for all of us is this - Are we receiving the nourishment and life offered by Christ? If not, we are missing a very special gift. We are missing some very special nourishment that will strengthen our branches and help us bear fruit, fruit that will last.

Maybe you are thinking you could use some more fertilizer to help your branches grow. Seek out the gardener, seek out Jesus Christ, and ask Him for more. Get into the handbook, the Bible for directions.

Prayer Time

Lord, help me to recognize where I fall short in my fruit bearing. Help me to strengthen my branches, to strengthen my connection to you, and to draw closer to the vine that gives life to me. Lord, thanks for your love every day. To you be the glory for my fruit tree. In your son's name I pray, Amen.

The Gardener

For those who are action thriller folks, the Gardener 7 is in a theatre near you. Gardener 7 or 007 for those who loved James Bond is here now, and He is doing His thing every day. Ok, I am stretching this thing I know. :) I was desperate for originality. Let's get serious shall we.

Who is the Gardener you ask? Let me share some things about Him.

What happens every single day in this world?

It happens no matter what time zone.

The sun rises and sets every day. Daily, God sends the sun and the rain to help crops grow. He is constantly nurturing the little plants and preparing them to blossom. It is so exciting when the crop finally reaches full bloom and has produced a harvest! It is the same thing with us, the branches. How exciting is it for God when we produce fruit?

John 15:8 says, "This is to my Father's glory, that you bear much fruit, showing yourselves to be my disciples."

When we live in a daily relationship with the gardener, in essence we are being watered and nurtured, so we too, can blossom and produce fruit, fruit that will last. Through that fruit, God will be glorified, and we will be His disciples.

Prayer Time

Lord, thank you for being the gardener in our lives. May our crops explode into a golden harvest, bringing honor and glory to you Lord. In Jesus' name I pray, Amen.

Wasted Fruit

Waste – it is a big deal. Every day in society, we waste. We produce, we present, we taste, and we waste. We waste opportunities.

Great opportunities come along and sometimes we waste them. I do not have all the answers as to why, but we do. Some say we have become a throwaway society. My brothers and I wasted many fruit during our fruit battles in the alley behind our house.

It is the same thing with bearing fruit for Jesus. We bear fruit, but how often do we waste it? How often does it go unaffected, or affect people lives? Is the fruit you are bearing making a difference?

Think of it this way - When I go to the store, I look for the most appealing fruit. I do not want to buy the unripened, nasty looking one, the one with big dents, odd shapes, and funny looking colors. I want the best one. I am thumping the melon, listening for the sound of ripeness. I will admit it, I have no idea what a ripe sound is on a melon, but I look masterful standing there.

When people look at us, will they see big dents, odd shapes, immature fruit, or will they see fruit that is appealing, something they want? Will they wonder who the gardener was when they look at our fruit, when they look at us? Will they want the fruit we have to offer? Will the fruit we have to offer be fruit that glorifies God, or will it glorify you and society?

Prayer Time

Lord, this morning my prayer is that we would not be wasteful. My prayer is the fruit we produce would be useful, fulfilling, appealing, and something someone would want. My prayer is the world would want to know who our gardener is. In your son's name I pray, Amen.

The Triumphal Entry

John 12:13-19: "The next day the large crowd that had come to the feast heard that Jesus was coming to Jerusalem. So they took branches of palm trees and went out to meet him. They began to shout, "Hosanna! Blessed is the one who comes in the name of the Lord! Blessed is the king of Israel!" Jesus found a young donkey and sat on it, just as it is written, "Do not be afraid, people of Zion; look, your king is coming, seated on a donkey's colt!" (His disciples did not understand these things when they first happened, but when Jesus was glorified, then they remembered that these things were written about him and that these things had happened to him.) So the crowd who had been with him when he called Lazarus out of the tomb and raised him from the dead were continuing to testify about it. Because they had heard that Jesus had performed this miraculous sign, the crowd went out to meet him. Thus the Pharisees said to one another, "You see that you can do nothing. Look, the world has run off after him!"

Notice how the crowd followed Him. They had seen the miracle with Lazarus. Everyone was so excited to roll out the red carpet for His triumphal entry. However, several days later, their devotion proved to be short lived.

It was based on popularity and curiosity. They did nothing to stop His crucifixion a few days later.

Aren't you glad that God does not go by popularity or curiosity, that His devotion is everlasting and true? He loves you very much. That is NOT short lived.

Prayer Time

Father, I thank you that you are truly devoted to me despite my actions, faults, failures, or shortcomings. Father, help me to draw closer to you every day, and give me the strength to overcome the temptation to view you in worldly fashions that are short lived, surface, and curious. In Jesus' name, I pray. Amen.

I Can Do All Things

This morning I woke up with the song playing in my mind, "I can do all things through Christ who gives me strength, and I don't have to be strong enough....." Have you heard that song on a Christian radio station?

Have you ever prayed for people you do not know?

Today, I am asking you to pray for your fellow brothers and sisters. There are some real battles going on. They are in some serious battles with the enemy today, and they need your prayers. They need strength.

For those of you going through the battle right now, what are some of the things you need to fight? Paul gives us a list in Ephesians 6. He says we need a helmet, breastplate, sword, and a shield.

Would you go into battle without protection?

No! If you did, you would more than likely be killed. You don't enter a battle unarmed, correct?

Ephesians 6:10-18 tells us what we need to fight the battles in our lives. Please look at those verses and suit up.

My friends please remember that you are not alone in this life. Jesus Christ longs to be your comforter. He longs to love you, help you, defend you, and carry you in your times of trouble.

Have you heard of the verse that says, "I can do all things through Christ who gives me strength?" You can get through this, and you will.

Why go into battle alone when you can draw on the strength of Jesus Christ, your Lord and Savior?

Prayer Time

Please pray with me, "Lord, today, there are some real battles taking place. There are some real fights happening among your children. Father, I pray they would get into your Word and draw comfort from it. I pray they would get into your Word and draw wisdom, strength, peace, and love.

Lord, today's battles with the enemy are very real, and we need the full armor of God to protect us. We need you Lord, we need you. We cannot do this life without you. Some of us need to realize that we cannot go through this life without you, and we need you.

Today Lord, I am asking you to open my heart and mind so I can draw more of you in to help me overcome the trials in my life. I need wisdom to know what to do. I am lost, I am afraid, and I am broken. Jesus, please come and help me. Forgive me my sins, whatever they may be, and cleanse me anew. Strengthen me I pray, today. In Jesus' name, I pray all these things, Amen."

If you have prayed that prayer with me today, trust God for the answers. Trust God and know that He heard you today, get into His Word, and read all about His promises today.

You will be glad you did!

What is a Battle?

I was standing in front of the sink one morning after sending out an email and had a thought. Some of you might have been asking yourself what a battle is. Let's make this part two of the previous devotional for those who do not know.

A battle, to sum it up is - anything you find yourself struggling with, and it is creating pain, stress, unhappiness, and disconnect in your life.

There are all kinds of battles, and they are very real. You may be struggling with an addiction such as alcohol or drugs. It might be a medical situation, or a disagreement with a friend, or family member. It may be an anger issue. You may be going through difficulties with your child or children. Maybe your marriage is in trouble right now, or there is someone at work giving you a hard time. It could be financial.

You see, battles come in many different shapes and sizes. They present themselves in many different ways. It is how you arm yourself, and how you handle it that is going to help you get through the battle, and win the war. What are some of the ways you can do that?

1. Get into Gods Word. Everything we need to know is in there.

2. Talk to God and tell Him your struggles and your hurts. Do not think He already knows because He is God.

He wants to hear you say it aloud so He knows that you know.

 3. Tell a trusted friend who isn't going to gossip about your situation, one that will pray for you, and lift you up.

4. Go to a counselor or a group meeting if your situation requires it.

Be careful on trying to carry these burdens by yourself. Think about those things you are struggling with, and ask yourself if those are areas the enemy is really playing with right now.

See, the enemy does not go after lost people. Why? They are already lost; he has them right where he wants them - far from God. He goes after people who believe in Jesus Christ and he causes problems in their lives so they quit seeking God. He wants them to blame God. He longs for them to ruin their witness. That is the enemy's job.

The Bible says Satan prowls around like a roaring lion. 1 Peter 5:8-9: "Be sober and alert. Your enemy the devil, *like a roaring lion,* is on the prowl looking for someone to devour. Resist him, strong in your faith, because you know that your brothers and sisters throughout the world are enduring the same kinds of suffering. "

I want you to know you are not alone and do not need to be as you are going through these trials and tribulations. We have someone in our corner and his name is Jesus Christ. We have others as well who can relate to our suffering. We need to push through and claim the promises God has for us.

I apologize for the length of today's prayer for you, but I thought it was important to go over. My prayer for you is that you will get through the battles unharmed as possible. My prayer for you is that healing will start TODAY. My prayer is that you feel Gods love surround you.

Listen, we have the ability to hope in Jesus. I do not know about you, but that is whom I put my hope in. My prayer is that you will put your hope in Him and trust Him as you go through these difficult times. Praise God for those who are doing well right now.

Prayer Time

We thank you Lord and we praise your name. Please walk with us each day, and help us to rely on you, in lieu of our own strength. Amen.

Stop Horsey Stop!

Some years back my friends and I rented horses. I have always been nervous on a horse and I guess they know it, because they do not like me much.

We were trotting in the wooded areas of Loxahatchee, Florida. For those who do not know, its west of West Palm Beach. Anyway, we were trotting alongside a wooden fence that ran down the side of a canal. I was bringing up the rear and quite happy with the speed and position.

For some reason, my horse liked to run. He was not satisfied with a trot. I was more than satisfied with trotting, but he did not care what I did or thought. And so we started to gallop - and gallop -and gallop!!

"Stop horsey stop," and whipping him with a feather stick didn't make a dent in his gallop! Before I knew, we went from a gallop to whatever jockeys call FAST, and I held on for dear life - true story.

I had now passed my party, headed for a wooden fence up ahead that blocked you from going into the canal. My options were to jump off (fall off – as there would not be anything graceful at full speed) or stay on, and hope he would stop. There was another option I briefly considered - ride to the fence, jump like a champion horse, land with gracefulness, and dump in the canal. Last but not least, there was the option of riding through the fence. None of the options consisted of a graceful exit.

I do not know what happened, but all of a sudden my horse slowed down, reared up on his two back legs, spun around, and made an abrupt turn, stage right, and immediately took me to the fence that we had been riding next to. This is where I decided my horse was possessed and I had stayed on too long, and so I bailed.

The horse was much happier now that he had my lard bottom off his back, and he stood there eating grass as if nothing happened. I on the other hand, needed to change my pants.

There was no riding him back to the stables. I walked him all the way back, with my friends riding alongside.

I am reminded of how sometimes we can be as stubborn as the horse. We will do what we want to do, and we will sometimes run on ahead of God, thinking we know better than Him. He calls our name and we ignore Him. And it's when we see a dead end, or we see trouble ahead, that we stop suddenly, rear up and dump the rider. And then we act as if nothing happened. God comes along, grabs our bit, and walks us back to the stable to try again. The whole way back He does not scold us, He lovingly walks us back, loving on us the whole way.

Psalms 136:26 says, "Give thanks to the God of heaven, for his loyal love endures!"

Prayer Time

Father, I thank you for sparing my life that day. It could have turned out much worse for me. Thank you for leading me and loving me despite my running ahead of you.

I pray Lord that if anyone is on a fast horse going in the wrong direction, they will turn back and hear your voice. May everyone be blessed today. In Jesus' name I pray, Amen.

The Dwight Howard Story

We all know Dwight Howard. If you do not know who Dwight Howard is, you have not been watching any basketball or paying attention to what happened in Orlando, Florida.

Pretend with me for a moment you do know who Dwight Howard is (former center for The Orlando Magic).

In a previous message, I shared Matthew 7, where Jesus talks about really knowing Him. I mentioned that relationship with Jesus is essential. Today, I want to expand on that with an example you might relate.

I know Dwight Howard. I know his stats. I know his percentage of free throws, how many rebounds he makes in a game. I know how tall he is, and how long he was a Magic player. I know what kind of car he drives and where he lives. I also know that he has been in the news a lot lately. His name can be found very easily when I Google. He is well known in Orlando. I have been following his career and can tell you all the things he has done in basketball. I even tell people about him and recommend people watch him play basketball on TV. Dwight Howard has done some amazing things in his career.

Knowing all this, I decide to go visit Dwight Howard at his home. I knock on his door and his butler answers. With a home that big, he needs help caring for it. After all, he is Dwight Howard. His butler answers the door and I ask to enter. I want to see Dwight. I want to hang out with him for the day, eat his Doritos, and drink Mountain Dew. He will have the big bags no doubt, and tall cups. After all, I know all these things about him.

The butler says to me, "How do you know Mr. Howard?"

I reply, "I know all his statistics, etc. etc."

He then asks, "What is his favorite food for breakfast? What is his favorite childhood memory as a kid? Where did his father grow up? What was his mother's middle name? What does he like to do as a favorite past time in addition to basketball? What was the most meaningful thing that happened to him in high school?"

My response, "But I told people about how awesome a player he is. I have been following his stats and his career for years. Come on butler man, let me in!"

And with one swoop, the door closes in my face. I stand there thinking to myself, "I guess I'm not going to share those Doritos with Dwight huh?" Nope! Why?

Do you see what I am getting at here? Sure, I knew all the surface things about Dwight Howard. I have heard all these things in the news, out in public, and from other people. I have told people they need to watch Dwight play basketball. He's Superman! But I have never actually sat down with Dwight Howard and learned who the man really is. I cannot answer any of those questions. Why? It's because I do not know him personally. I do not have a relationship with him.

It is the same thing with Jesus. The people heard all the stories. Some even saw the miracles for themselves. Some even prophesied in His name. (Matthew 7), but did they know Jesus as their personal Lord and Savior? Did they build a relationship with Him, and draw close to Him? Are we doing that?

You say, "Well, I don't know how. I don't really know where to begin and how to build a relationship with Jesus."

1. Start in God's Word. God is so awesome; He gave us the Bible, His Word. It is the inside scoop on everything you want to know about His son, Jesus Christ. You can read in the Old Testament many prophecies about the Son of God coming. Read in the New Testament how those prophecies came true. The book of John is a great place to start. John outlines the details of Jesus' life, perhaps the most out of the four gospels.

 2. Get to know Jesus and ask Him straight out to help you draw closer to Him. Pray that He will reveal Himself to you. Spend time in prayer with Him.

Tell Jesus everything. Treat Him as you would your best friend. You tell them everything, tell Jesus everything. He is not judgmental, low on grace or too busy. He is available all the time. You might be saying, "But you don't know what I've done or I don't want to start now.

Jesus is not like that. Now is as good a time as any and time is ticking away.

Jesus Christ is the key. A relationship with Him is an essential part of our foundation on this earth. It is the base on which you build everything else. If you do not have a firm foundation, life gets very shaky. Jesus Christ is that base, that firm foundation. It is like building on concrete, instead of sand.

Prayer Time

Father, I pray if anyone reading this does not know where to start with building a relationship with your son, Jesus, that you would reveal it to them. Your Word is full of love, direction, stories about your son and the miracles He did. It also shares the sacrifice He made for each one of us when He died on the cross for our sins. Help us to get to know Him better and build a relationship with Him that will far exceed anything we know in this life. All these things I pray in your son's name, Amen.

Finally, do not ask me for Dwight Howard's stats. I have no idea. Sorry.

Faith of the Centurion

We have been talking about a relationship with Jesus and having Him as your firm foundation.

Today, I want to share with you something that is very important. Today's passage comes from Matthew 8. Yes, we are still in Matthew.

Matthew 8:5-13: "When he entered Capernaum, a centurion came to him asking for help: "Lord, my servant is lying at home paralyzed, in terrible anguish." Jesus said to him, "I will come and heal him. "But the centurion replied, "Lord, I am not worthy to have you come under my roof. Instead, just say the word and my servant will be healed. For, I too am a man under authority, with soldiers under me. I say to this one, 'Go' and he goes, and to another 'Come' and he comes, and to my slave 'Do this' and he does it." When Jesus heard this, he was amazed and said to those who followed him, "I tell you the truth, I have not found such faith in anyone in Israel! I tell you, many will come from the east and west to share the banquet with Abraham, Isaac, and Jacob in the kingdom of heaven, but the sons of the kingdom will be thrown out into the outer darkness, where there will be weeping and gnashing of teeth." Then Jesus said to the centurion, "Go; just as you believed, it will be done for you." And the servant was healed at that hour."

A centurion, for those of you who do not know was a career military officer in the Roman army with control over a hundred soldiers. Roman soldiers of all people were hated by the Jews for their oppression, control, and ridicule. Yet this man's genuine faith amazes Jesus. He was a hated Gentile by the Jews. In verse 11, Jesus is referring to the four corners of the world from which all the faithful will come and feast with the Messiah. However, there will be those who will be excluded because they put their religious traditions ahead of Christ and His message. In this passage, Matthew is referring to the religious Jews and Jewish leaders.

What we have to remember is that the message from Jesus is for everyone. It is universal. It is for you, me, the Jew, the gentile, purple, yellow, brown, black, white, red, and green. The Old Testament prophets knew this message was for everyone, but the Jewish leaders of the New Testament chose to ignore it. Each individual has to choose to accept or reject the gospel, and no one can become part of God's kingdom based on heritage or connections. You must believe and follow Christ.

How do we do that? It starts with admitting Jesus Christ is Lord. You must believe He died on the cross for your sins and that you are a sinner. Then you must confess your sin and ask Him to come into your heart to live. Once you have prayed those things, you will have become a child of God. From there, you walk in relationship with Jesus Christ on a daily basis.

Prayer Time

Father God, you know us all intimately, every detail, every hair on our heads. God, open our eyes to see your glory. Open our hearts to receive your love. Open our arms that we may embrace you. Open our minds so that we can grasp it, and help us Lord to build a relationship, so deep, so pure, so sweet with your son, Jesus. If it were not for Him, I would not have a chance. It would be as an old friend of mine used to say, "I'd be gagging on gnats and swallowing camels." I would be a mess Lord if you were not the one in control of my life. It is difficult knowing there are many out there who do not believe in you. Lord God, I pray for changed hearts and minds today. I claim your promises today. I love you with all of me. In Jesus' name, I pray all these things, Amen.

Joy in Trials

James 1:2-8: "My brothers and sisters, consider it nothing but joy when you fall into all sorts of trials, because you know that the testing of your faith produces endurance. And let endurance have its perfect effect, so that you will be perfect and complete, not deficient in anything. But if anyone is deficient in wisdom, he should ask God, who gives to all generously and without reprimand, and it will be given to him. But he must ask in faith without doubting, for the one who doubts, is like a wave of the sea, blown and tossed around by the wind. For that person must not suppose that he will receive anything from the Lord, since he is a double-minded individual, unstable in all his ways."

I do not know about you, but there was a time in my life when I shuttered at the word, trials. Trials were a problem - they were stressful, and most of the time they cost me, whether it be time or money. Trials were no fun. You are probably agreeing with me right now or thinking, "I'm in the midst of trials right now. There is no "used to be" for me right now. They are no fun!!"

Check out the following footnote: "The author of this passage, James, who was Jesus' brother, wrote this letter to some early Christian believers. Stephen had been martyred, and James felt these people needed some extra encouragement."

They did not have established churches back then, so he wrote this letter to them to show support. What is interesting is that James does not say, "*If* you face trials," he says "*when* you fall into all sorts of trials", meaning you will face trials of many kinds and it is possible to benefit from them. We do not want to go around pretending to be happy, but we do want to try to have a joyful outlook during these hard times because good things can come out of them. If you really look at what you are going through, something good is coming out of it. It may not be what you pictured or hoped for, but something is happening.

Tough times teach us perseverance. It is in these times, we see what we are really made of. Can we endure? Can we make it? Can we help someone else? We can, but we have to believe.

We have a heavenly Father who promises to be with us during tough times. Thank God for that. Can you imagine going through this life by yourself? I sure can't. I am so thankful every day that I do not have to manage problems by myself. I have the free will to ask God for wisdom, to ask Him for help, and then to be patient as I wait for that help. How hard is that sometimes? For me, patience is not one of my virtues. I want His answers and help right now, today! But I have to trust that God knows better than me, and is working in my situation, and the outcome will be far greater than anything I could have come up with on my own.

Wisdom is the ability to make wise decisions in difficult situations, and James is talking about having knowledge. Whenever we need wisdom, ask God for some. You do not need a phone, a text, or email. We do not have to wait in line. We do not have to go to an office. We do not have to stumble around in the dark, hoping to find it. We have the ability to ask Him right now, today.

Prayer Time

Lord, I pray for wisdom. Like Solomon, Lord, who asked for wisdom, that is my prayer. People are going through many trials, and I pray Lord you bring them wisdom for their circumstances. Help us all to make the right decisions in these difficult times. Lord, it is comforting to know we do not have to go through this life alone. We have you. Help us to lean on you today Lord. Give us the wisdom to do so. Everything I pray in your son's name, Amen.

Dig Deeper

Today, I am going back to James 1 to dig deeper into what he had to say. Obviously, God felt that James had some very meaningful things to say or He would not have it included them in His inspired Word, the Bible, for all to read and meditate on. So with that, let's get down to business.

Verse 5 says, "If any of you lacks wisdom, he should ask God, who gives generously to all without finding fault, and it will be given to him."

How many of you have asked someone for something only to get a condition attached to it or a speech? "I'm going to do this for you, but remember when you did...... and you said you would do......and I haven't seen......."

If you recall from the previous pages, I said God will give generously if we ask it. We do not have to feel around in the dark as if trying to find a hidden treasure. He gives it freely. We are talking about wisdom, not a winning lottery ticket. I have heard many people say winning the lottery would be the answer to all their problems. I do not know about you, but I have not heard too many positive outcomes from winners of the lottery. It could be the media does not report those stories or know of them.

Let us look at wisdom as having three distinct characteristics and I am not talking about shoe size, dress length, and hairstyle. When going out for a special evening, yes, those are all nice characteristics, but we are talking about an everyday thing here.

1. It is practical. What does that mean? First thing I think of when I think practical is it makes sense or it is easy. A deeper definition might be that wisdom from God relates to life even during the most trying times. I can apply wisdom to any circumstance or trial I face. Wisdom is the tool by which trials are overcome. It gives me comfort knowing I have that available to me, and I do not have to know physics. God bless you if you do.

Intelligence will allow someone to give you several reasons why the car broke down, but the wise person chooses the most likely reason and proceeds to fix it. Go back to my analogy on Dwight Howard. I can tell you all the stats on him, but what I really need to know to sit down and eat Doritos with the guy is what I should know and put into action.

2. It is divine. Someone once asked me what I thought of their chocolate cake. I responded, "It's divine." This point is a little different from that. God's wisdom goes beyond common sense. Common sense is not something I use to choose joy in the midst of a trial. This wisdom begins with respect for God, leads to living by God's direction and results in my ability to tell right from wrong.

3. It is Christ like - How is it Christ like? It is ultimately asking to be more like Christ. How is asking for wisdom ultimately asking to be more like Christ? I do not know about you, but when I think of Christ, I think of a smart man, a wise man, and a God filled man. He came to this earth, was tempted in the same ways as you and I, and

he never sinned. His example is one I should be pulling from, not something that changes all the time.

In 1 Corinthians 1:24 and again in 2:1-7, the Bible describes Christ as the "wisdom of God."

The question is - what will you do with wisdom? How will you proceed?

Prayer Time

Lord, today as we talked about wisdom, God I pray for wisdom. Lord, I have no idea what I am doing, but I have trusted you, followed your Word, and doing my best to make wise decisions in difficult situations.

In a world full of choices, ideas and solutions, help me Lord to choose the one that best follows you and your Word. Help me Lord to focus on you and not the solutions that bring instant gratification. I have learned Father over the years, instant gratification is just that, but the residual fall out lasts a lot longer.

Thank you Lord, for the unending love and mercy you have showed me. Lord, be with us today and in your son's name I pray all these things, Amen.

Squirrels – Really?

My favorite little animal is the squirrel. They are so cute, yet sometimes I wonder if they have a brain in their head. The question comes to mind quite often as I see them lying dead in the middle of the road. Of course, I cannot stand seeing that. Ask my daughter how many times she got close to whiplash from mom slamming on the brakes to stop and move their lifeless bodies out of the street. If I were lying dead in the middle of the road, I would want someone to stop and move me to the side in lieu of vehicles purposely trying to make me a permanent part of the pavement.

However, when you reflect on their lives, to me they are no different from you or me. They too, were created by God. They have a heart. They were born as little babies, their mommas fed them, and they grew up, and are now making their own decisions. They have to feed their families, find shelter, avoid evil and troublesome situations, and some day they too will die. Some will make costly mistakes and lose their lives. Others will eat themselves into frenzy.

Still others will catch diseases that will end their lives prematurely. I bet you did not realize how much you had in common with the squirrels everyone takes aim at driving down the street playing the game, chicken!

Do not misunderstand what I am saying; I am not saying we evolved from them. :)

The other day while driving, I saw a few squirrels in the grassy area on the side of the road. They were digging for food and a thought came to mind. Look at how God has provided for them. They are being cared for. They have shelter in the trees. If you notice, you never see them at night, so they must be tucked away in their little homes for the evening. They have each other to play and frolic with, chasing each other and jumping from tree to tree. They have amazing skill. If God can take care of the squirrels and provide for them, surely He takes care of and provides for us. Therefore, do not worry.

It says in Matthew 6:25-34: "Therefore I tell you, do not worry about your life, what you will eat or drink, or about your body, what you will wear. Isn't there more to life than food and more to the body than clothing? Look at the birds in the sky: They do not sow, or reap, or gather into barns, yet your heavenly Father feeds them. Aren't you more valuable than they are? And which of you by worrying can add even one hour to his life? Why do you worry about clothing? Think about how the flowers of the field grow; they do not work or spin. Yet I tell you that not even Solomon in all his glory was clothed like one of these! And if this is how God clothes the wild grass, which is here today and tomorrow is tossed into the fire to heat the oven, won't he clothe you even more, you people of little faith? So then don't worry saying, 'What will we eat?' or 'What will we drink?' or 'What will we wear?' For the unconverted pursue these things, and your heavenly Father knows that you need them. But above all pursue his kingdom and righteousness, and all these things will be given to you as well. So then, do not worry about tomorrow, for tomorrow will worry about itself. Today has enough trouble of its own."

Isn't it comforting to know that God will and does take care of us like He does the birds of the air and the squirrels on the ground?

What are you worried about today?

Hand it over to God, go frolic, and play in the trees. (Well, not literally, but you know what I mean).

Prayer Time

Father God, I am so thankful you take care of me. Lord, you know how many times, like a squirrel, I ran out in front of trouble only to incur injury. You nursed me back; you cared for and provided for me. Like the birds of the air, you feed me too.

You have given us your Word as nourishment to our bodies, food to eat, sustenance for everlasting life. Lord, help us to put our trust in you and be confident that what your Word says, you do.

Lord, if there are some reading this today, who care about squirrels and other small animals, may they too stop and move them out of the roadway. It sure would save the county workers and me some time. In Jesus' name I pray, Amen.

Birds on the Wire

I often take a short stroll outside in the morning to look up, thank my Lord for another day, His beautiful sky, and then listen. I listen for the beautiful sound of birds speaking to each other. It amazes me they can understand each other's call, and each bird sounds different.

As I am driving to work each morning, I am always amazed at the birds sitting on the high wires above - the cable, the phone, and the power lines.

Do they have any idea how much information is passing beneath their feet? Do they know how fast the world is going by underneath them? The world's information is traveling so quickly from place to place. Emails we are sending and receiving are passing beneath them, and they do not have a clue.

If you notice, the birds have all figured out which lines to sit on. Years ago, Harry the pigeon, landed on the hot wire and he was toast. Word got around quickly. He set the tone and example for the rest of them – "ok, we now know NOT to land on *those* wires."

Let's think about the raven. Ravens for the most part are plain birds. They have no fancy feathers, no spectacular colors. They do not stand out in a pretty display at the zoo. They are just ravens, nothing special to look at. They lack skill and beauty unlike the blue jay, the woodpecker, or even the canary. They are just plain birds, yet they get the attention of the Psalmist in Psalm

67

147:9 where it says, "He provides food to the cattle and for the young ravens when they call."

Maybe today, you are not feeling very special, maybe you're feeling unremarkable, forgotten, or lacking special skills. You might think of yourself as plain, all black feathers in a world full of vibrant colors. Why would God answer your call? Maybe you are thinking you have nothing to offer God or anyone.

This verse assures us that God does hear our call to Him, our cry, and our prayer. He does not respond based on how spectacular we are or not. He does not respond based on what we have to offer Him. He responds because we are His children, plain and simple. He responds because it is in His nature to respond. We must believe that with all our hearts and stand on the truth as we wait for the response.

Isn't it funny how the ravens always cry out, sing out and wait, knowing their call will be answered? They wait with confidence.

Maybe we should be more like the ravens and sing out with confidence that our Lord, our loving, Heavenly Father will hear us and wait. I have always heard God's timing is not our timing and His ways are not our ways. The Bible tells me so. Look it up, I believe there is a verse that says so.

Prayer Time

Lord, help me to have the confidence the ravens have to sing out to you, knowing I have been heard. Help me to wait patiently on you Lord as you work in my life and others. And Lord, help me to be as smart as birds, to figure out which lines to sit on and which lines to avoid, especially in the grocery store.

Be with those reading this. Father, put your loving arms around them and assure them of your presence. Like the raven, God, I am plain and you love me just the same. For that, I am thankful and pray in Jesus' name, Amen.

Comfort

Today it is all about comfort.

2 Corinthians 1:3-4: "Blessed is the God and Father of our Lord Jesus Christ, the Father of mercies and God of all comfort, who comforts us in all our troubles so that we may be able to comfort those experiencing any trouble with the comfort with which we ourselves are comforted by God. "

Comfort is something we all need and isn't it wonderful that God thought we did too, and had a plan for it? The footnote in my Bible says, "Many people think when God comforts us, our trials should go away. If that were the case, then we would only seek God in the midst of trials."

It would be like coming through the storm and then saying to God, "Thanks. I'll see you around some time. I am good now, I don't need you. You can go help someone else."

You see, we should desire to turn to God at all times, whether going through pain or joyful times. Our eyes should always be on Him.

Being comforted should also mean receiving strength, encouragement, and hope to endure the hard times that come our way. The more we suffer, the more God comforts us.

Do not forget every trial we suffer is another opportunity to help comfort others who will endure trials as well.

If you are suffering right now and need comfort, allow God to comfort you. Do not think, "He doesn't have time, He's too busy with others, or it's so small, I don't want to bother Him." I have heard those before.

Do you think God is too busy for you or He does not know what is going on? "He is able, more than able, to handle anything that comes my way. He is able, more than able"...those are a few lines of the song, He is able! My God is able to handle it, trust me!

Do you trust God to handle it? Will you ask Him to comfort you today?

Prayer Time

Father God, there are many things going on with everyone, some more than others. There are people in pain, some we know about, some we do not. But I take heart Lord, because you know all of them, and you know them by name.

Today God, as they make their way through their day, may they reach out to you for comfort. May they rest in you, and may you give them strength, endurance, and hope to get through the trying times. They may think they are not capable of receiving, they may think they are not capable of handling it, but God you know they can and you are there with them. May you be glorified through their trial. All these things I ask in your son's name, Amen. And all God's people said? Amen

The River

Blessings to you! If you have not been outside to listen to the birds tweet a lullaby, take a few minutes and check them out. It is the little things in this life that can bring such peace.

Today I want to share a verse with you from Isaiah 43:2 which says, "When you pass through the waters, I will be with you, and when you pass through the rivers, they will not sweep over you. When you walk through the fire, you will not be burned; the flames will not set you ablaze."

What is the prophet Isaiah saying here?

Quite simply, when you are feeling overwhelmed, God is there with power to help you. Alone you will drown in deep waters of difficulty; with God, you will prevail over floods or fires.

Apply this to something we all see on television.

Northerners deal with flash flooding from time to time, probably more often than they would like. What you will notice is the person being carried away by those waters, alone, they struggle. But if they have help, if they hang onto something substantial which helps them float, most of the time, they make it safely to dry ground. If they operated on their own strength, they were not as successful. When there were other people around, they were more likely to be rescued.

If you invite the Lord into your difficult situation, into the river or fire in your life, you can draw from His power, not your own.

I love this analogy: I like my toaster to toast garlic bread. But if I do not plug it into the power, it is useless, it will not toast at all. I must plug into Gods power to reap the full benefit. If I do not plug in or draw from His strength, things in this life are not going to work very well, and I am going to find I struggle a lot more.

Make sense?

Prayer Time

Father God, I am so thankful you are there to help me and you want to help me. You go with me as I pass through those deep waters. You are with me through the blazes in this life, and each time I go through them, I come out stronger. I come out more refined, more ready to face them again.

I thank you for your power. I thank you that your power is free to me. I do not have to pay a huge deposit to get it turned on. I do not have to pay a monthly bill to keep it turned on. Your power is unending. All I have to do is seek you and reside in your love, in you.

Let us draw from your power, your strength as we face difficult challenges in our lives, as we face the raging rivers and firestorms in our lives. In Jesus, whom we can put all our hope and trust in, Amen. And all God's people said? _____

My Weakness

Today, I want to talk about weakness. For many months, I dealt with leg pain resulting from a herniated L4/L5 disc. Because of the leg pain, I became weak. There were many nights I begged God to take the pain away. I spent a lot of time in doctor offices. My poor wallet reflects how many times I heard the word co-pay and deductible. Come to think of it, it is still experiencing the pains of co-pay and deductible having had the surgery to repair the problem.

That is a minute problem now and the benefits of getting help. But now I can give a big shout out for the relief. I thank my Lord for the wonderful blessing of not being in any more pain.

There were days I felt like Paul. I read in 2 Corinthians 12:6-10 the following passage and oh, how I could relate to him when I was in pain:

"For even if I wish to boast, I will not be a fool, for I would be telling the truth, but I refrain from this so that no one may regard me beyond what he sees in me or what he hears from me, even because of the extraordinary character of the revelations. Therefore, so that I would not become arrogant, a thorn in the flesh was given to me, a messenger of Satan to trouble me – so that I would not become arrogant. I asked the Lord three times about this, that it would depart from me. But he said to me, "My grace is enough for you, for my power is made perfect in weakness." So then, I will boast most gladly about my weaknesses, so that the power of Christ may reside in me. Therefore I am content with weaknesses, with insults, with troubles, with persecutions and difficulties for the sake of Christ, for whenever I am weak, then I am strong."

There are times when we cannot understand why God does not take our pain away, but we know our weaknesses are great opportunities for God to do amazing things and work His power through us.

The Bible does not say what Paul's thorn was. There have been many assumptions made by men, but no one really knows. What we do know, is while he did not receive an answer to his prayer to have the thorn removed, what he did receive was even greater. He became stronger. He received greater grace, humility and the ability to empathize with others.

I learned some of those same things during the whole season of my life with my disc herniation. I have a healthy, new appreciation for the handicapped. I empathize with people in wheelchairs, those who use canes, walkers, and motorized scooters. Theirs is not an easy life. The braces people must use and adapt to are not easy either. At one time or another during those painful months, I had to use one of those apparatuses and all those things humbled me.

I wanted God to take my pain away, but instead I received far greater blessings from having it.

Today, I am limited in what I can do physically, but I am not limited mentally. I can do far greater things for the Lord than I could do before. God, according to His sovereign plan, does not heal some believers of their physical ailments, and we do not always know why. However, one thing God will do and has promised is to demonstrate His power through us.

Prayer Time

Lord, we do not understand it, especially when it involves ourselves or someone we love. But Lord, the one thing I keep holding onto is- you do. And, you know all things. I can come to you and rest. Father, the prayer is as we come out of those difficult times, difficult seasons in our lives, we would continue to hold onto you and stay close. We have a tendency to move on when the storm calms.

Lord, help us to do your work, seek your face, and rest in your comfort, your peace, and your ability to carry us through; even when the road gets rough, the storms of life get dark and gloomy. You are the light which shines on us all. You make your presence known and I know for me, I could not live without you. In your son's name I pray, Amen.

Weakness Part Two

In Part 1 on my thought about weakness, and I am summarizing here, God uses our weaknesses to make us strong. He will do, and has promised to demonstrate His power through us. Well, what does it mean exactly? How would God demonstrate His power through us?

Go back to the toaster for a moment. In order for me to toast garlic bread, I need the toaster and it needs power to work. I must plug it into the wall socket. Through the plug, the electric passes through to the toaster and ahoy, your toaster works. (I do not know how to spell wa la).

One thing to note - you control how much it toasts.

The current through the cord is the same, but you control the toaster by the settings. It is either going to come out golden brown or burnt like a crisp. I once knew an older man from twenty-five years ago who ate burnt toast every morning for breakfast. It helped his digestion. His teeth were not always the prettiest, but it was an easy fix-o-dent. I know I am going downhill quickly here. Get to the point Jeanette!

Although God did not remove Paul's thorn, He promised to demonstrate His power through him. When you read about the Apostle Paul's life, Gods power becomes very clear.

When we think about it, Gods power is displayed through weak people, through our weaknesses, and that should give us courage. Though we recognize our limitations, we are not here to congratulate ourselves, but to seek pathways for effectiveness. We must rely on God for our effectiveness. This is not a self-serving mission. We must rely on Him for our effectiveness rather than our own power, strength, abilities, or talents.

See, as the toaster must rely on the power coming from the cord plugged in (evidence you paid the bill); we have to rely on God's power to make us stronger and more effective. Otherwise, we are tempted to go it alone and think we can do it without Him.

God does not intend for us to be weaklings and ineffective. Every day, life provides enough setbacks and obstacles without us creating them. We must depend on God. Only His power will help make us effective for Him, and help us do work that has lasting value.

Lastly, our weakness does a few things: It helps develop Christian character. It deepens our worship, and in both of these things, God is glorified. By admitting we are weak, we affirm Gods strength.

What's the moral of the story? Allow God to fill you with His power, then you will be stronger then you could have ever been on your own.

Prayer Time

Lord, I am so thrilled to be filled with your power. Jesus Christ paid the power bill for me so I could have access to your power. And just like we have to call the power company to hook us up, we need to call on you, Lord, to fill us with your power. We need your power in us, to help us with our weaknesses and to glorify you in everything we do. I do not know about everyone else, but I would mess it up big time if I did not have you in my life, if I did not have your power to deal with the every day.

Help me to rest in the knowledge of knowing you can fill me up. All I have to do is ask and receive. In Philippians 4:13 it says, "I can do everything through Him who gives me strength." Thanks Lord for the promises and be with all those who are feeling weak, feeling overwhelmed, or fearful. May they find their power in you God. I pray these things in your son's name, Amen.

It was Time to Make the Donuts

"It's 5:30am, time to make the donuts"!

Do you remember the commercial from twenty- five plus years ago of the little, round guy who would drag himself out of bed each morning at 5:30 and say, "It's time to make the donuts, time to make the donuts?"

For those of you with no clue, it was a very famous commercial for Dunkin Donuts.

When you think of how he looked walking across the room, shoulders hunched over, walking very slow, looking like he had not slept in weeks, he looked how we feel some days.

We approach things some times in the same fashion, "it's time to ...." When we think we cannot go anymore, let me give you a little encouragement from Gods Word.

Isaiah 40:28-31: "Do you not know?" Have you not heard? The Lord is an eternal God, the creator of the whole earth. He does not get tired or weary; there is no limit to his wisdom. He gives strength to those who are tired; to the ones who lack power, he gives renewed energy. Even youths get tired and weary; even strong young men clumsily stumble. But those who wait for the Lord's help find renewed strength; they rise up as if they had eagles' wings, they run without growing weary, they walk without getting tired."

Some of you will recognize the lyrics of a popular song with a little boy who reads the Bible at the end. He was reading those words.

Isn't it a wonderful promise for you to hold onto today?

Listen, life is not as easy as getting up and making donuts. I'm sure some of us wouldn't mind trading in our current status for a donut hole, but take heart, we have more than flour and sugar in our midst. We have the glue which keeps it all together and forms us into a wonderful creation.

We have the Lord our God, who gives strength to the tired and power to those who are weak.

Stay steadfast loved ones and let us ask God together to be with us today.

Prayer Time

Father God, we thank you for being the source of strength, and for those of us who have not thought of you for strength, may we look to you now. Lord, help us draw from your power, your strength when we are in those moments of the day wondering how we will get through the next five minutes.

We thank you for your provisions in our lives. And of course Lord, some of us thank you for donuts. What a wonderful creation generated from basic food items created long ago from the ground.

Lord, help those who make them, figure out a way to make them less fattening, but just as good. Thanks Lord. In your son's name I pray, Amen.

Some of you may be asking, "How can you pray like that?" When God is my best friend, I can be myself. God has a sense of humor too you know. :) Smile, take heart, you are not alone!

Did you Hear me?

Ever applied for a position or a loan, or make a very important phone call, and then.......wait?

What about when you prayed to God? Did you pray and ask Him for specific answers and then........you wait?

The waiting becomes especially uncomfortable when we are in the midst of a dark time in our lives doesn't it? It seems like God takes forever to answer, and we ask, "God, did you hear me? God, have you left me? God, are you still there?"

Today's passage comes from Psalm 13:1-6:

"How long, Lord, will you continue to ignore me? How long will you pay no attention to me? How long must I worry, and suffer in broad daylight? How long will my enemy gloat over me? Look at me! Answer me, O Lord my God! Revive me, or else I will die! Then my enemy will say, "I have defeated him!" Then my foes will rejoice because I am upended. But I trust in your faithfulness. May I rejoice because of your deliverance! I will sing praises to the Lord when he vindicates me."

Even David struggled with this. Actually, David struggled with this quite often, claiming God was slow to act on his behalf.

I am sure we feel the same way sometimes. It seems suffering and the evil in this world go unchecked, and we wonder where God is and when He will put a stop to it.

But we also know from reading scripture, David affirmed many times he would continue to trust God no matter how long it took, no matter how long he had to wait.

The other thing I would like for you to see from the above passage is David expressed his true feelings to God and he found strength. By the end of the prayer, if you notice, he rejoiced. He would sing praises. Through our prayers, we can express our true feelings to God and talk out our problems with Him. God will help us regain our strength, get the right perspective, and give us peace.

Moral of the story - Do not trust your feelings, trust God. Feelings will lead you to do lot of things, but having faith and waiting on the Lord will help you do the right thing.

Prayer Time

Lord, we come to you today, many waiting on answered prayer. While we wait, may we be patient, trusting in you Lord, that you are working all things together for the good of those who love you.

Father, we do not always have the answers. We do not always know the direction to take, but one thing I do know Lord - I can look up to you, tell you about my fears, my frustrations and anything else, and you DO hear me. Lord, help me. May your peace engulf me and draw me closer to you. In Jesus' name I pray, Amen.

It's not Even Noon yet!

Ever had one of those days when you say to yourself with frustration, "It's not even noon yet and I feel like I have handled a week worth of problems?"

I think we have all said that to ourselves at one time or another. I was thinking about when I feel like that some days, and then I multiplied the same feeling by millions, and my head blew up like a big balloon, popped, and my meatballs, I mean my good brain fell onto the floor.

God has to handle millions of prayer requests every single day before noon! Ok, I will give Him a little leeway and say He handles them all before noon in the different time zones, six hours here, eight hours ahead there, one hour back, Eastern, Central, and Pacific. LOL

But really when you think about it, my God can do all things Amen! And what is even more cool, is He gives me the strength to handle things that come my way too. He is not a greedy God, keeping all the strength to Himself.

Look at what Paul writes in Philippians 4:12-13:

"I know what it is to be in need, and I know what it is to have plenty. I have learned the secret of being content in any and every situation, whether well fed or hungry, whether living in plenty or in want. I can do everything through him who gives me strength."

The question is - Can we really do everything?

Loved ones, the power we receive in union with Christ is sufficient to do His will and to face the challenges that arise from our commitment to doing it. He is not going to make us into Superman or Cat Woman, with superhuman ability to accomplish anything we can without regards to His interests. Thank God because you do not want to see me in full-length tights. I am not so sure I want to see you in full-length tights either. :)

The point is, as we strive for the faith, we will face troubles, pressures, and trials, some of them before noon today. As we do though, ask Christ to strengthen you.

Prayer Time

Father God, it is a wonderful reassurance to us that we can call upon you for strength and you so freely give it. We do not have to slide a credit card through the machine. We do not have to dig change out of our pockets or wallets. We can just call on you.

Lord, today, we need your strength. We need to be filled up, so we can make it past noon and still have our brains intact from the pressure which will build. Help us Lord to rely on the strength you gave us, and not the devices we come up with.

In our own power, we are weak, but you are strong. What a blessing to have you in our lives and be able to draw from your power Father, every day. I pray Lord in your son's name, Amen.

Waiting with Anticipation

"When I was a young wart hog!!!!! When she was a young wart hog!!!"

Those words came to my mind when I started to tell a story from my childhood. I saw the Broadway musical, *Lion King* on a Broadway stage. If you consider the local stage where I live Broadway, then it qualifies. Let's start again. :)

When I was about twelve, my two brothers and I would string dads fishing line across the road, tying it from one phone pole to another at car windshield height. Then we would hide in the bushes, wait for an unsuspecting car to drive down the street, and through our make shift finish line. Success was ours when we heard the ping of the popped line.

Of course, at the time, we did not view it as a finish line so much, but more along the lines of them running into something. As I type this, I am asking myself what was so funny about this. What was so hilarious about a car driving through fishing line? Why did we sit in the bushes for what seemed like forever, flicking ants and other bugs off our bodies while we waited for our next unsuspecting victim?

Sometimes, we would wait for five minutes up to fifteen or twenty for a car to come by. And the whole time, we waited anxiously, giggling, sometimes picking at each other just to pass the time. But we would wait with great anticipation.

Other times we would take old clothes, fill them with wood, and lay them on the side of the road. Unsuspecting cars would drive by, slam on the brakes, take a double take, then speed off when they realized it was a fake person, a trick played by a couple of kids.

We would laugh. We thought it was so funny. Again, we waited with anticipation for something to happen. Again, I question why it was so funny. Remember people, I was twelve.

We had planned, we had taken all the steps, and then it was time to wait for the reaction, for the moment of satisfaction - the ping!

Fast-forward thirty-years and it is the same way. I plan, I work, I lay a foundation, and I wait. Only now, I have added prayer to my Heavenly Father as I do all these things and wait on Him. Sometimes, I will get the answer I am looking for, other times, I will not. Then there are times when I wait, and I wait, and I wait with great anticipation for Him to answer me. It is like waiting for ketchup to come out of the bottle.

Other times, He has answered me and I chose not to accept the answer because it was not what I wanted. It was Gods answer though, because He knew what was best for me.

Psalms 116:1-2 says, "I love the Lord because he hears and answers my prayers. Because he bends down and listens, I will pray as long as I have breath."

God always listens and responds to our prayers. But as a loving Heavenly Father who knows what is best, He does not always give us what we ask for.

If you are waiting on the side of the road, hiding in the bushes, waiting in anticipation for an answer to prayer, do not be discouraged. God is near. He has heard your prayer and our loving, Heavenly Father will answer your prayer according to what He feels is best for you. Our idea of what we think is best will not always line up with what God thinks is best for us. Sometimes it's a very good thing, believe me!

Prayer Time

Lord, I thank you for knowing what is best for me. By now I would have messed things up big time had I gone with what I thought was best for me.

I would not have reaped the fullness of this life, and what it had to offer living for you. Oh, this world has a lot to offer me, but that does not mean it is all good or beneficial.

Lord, I lift up my voice to you with prayer and petition. I wait patiently "in the bushes" for you to answer. Just like when I was twelve years old, I wait with anticipation for something great to happen, for your answer to my prayers. I will accept them, whether it is the answer I was looking for or what you feel was best for me. Either way, I wait and trust. In your son's name I pray, Amen.

A Little Guidance Please

2 Peter 1:2-4: "May grace and peace be lavished on you as you grow in the rich knowledge of God and of Jesus our Lord! I can pray this because his divine power has bestowed on us everything necessary for life and godliness through the rich knowledge of the one who called us by his own glory and excellence. Through these things he has bestowed on us his precious and most magnificent promises, so that by means of what was promised you may become partakers of the divine nature, after escaping the worldly corruption that is produced by evil desire."

Have you ever had to study for a big test? Maybe you do not remember how much dedication it took to get ready for the big exam. If we are going to pass the test and receive a good grade, we must study. We must invest our time. We must get to know the material so when exam day comes, we are fully prepared to answer as many questions correctly as we can to get the "A" we desire.

It is the same with God. Many believers want an abundance of God's grace and peace in their lives, but they are unwilling to put forth the effort it takes to get to know Him better. They are unwilling to study the textbook, the Bible, or meet with God in prayer.

Listen, listen. We cannot rely on our own power if we are to grow, because the power does not come from within - it comes from God.

How weak are we when we rely on our own power? One of the big reasons is because we do not have what it takes to be true godly people.

Verse four talks about "partaking of the divine nature." God allows us to "participate in the divine nature in order to keep us from sin and help us live for Him."

When we are born again, God, by His Spirit empowers us with His own moral goodness. You may be asking yourself right now, "What is moral goodness?" My answer - You can find the definition in the textbook, the Bible.

What will you do? Are you going to invest the time and energy it takes and get the "A" or will you slide by and be satisfied with a satisfactory, "at least I passed" type grade?

It is too easy these days to go with the flow, to float downstream with everyone else, because it seems right, it feels easy. Everyone else is floating down stream too. "Get your tube, let's just float. I'm tired." But is it wonderful? Where does the river end? Is it the river of worldly corruption, or one of peace and blessings from God? Are you floating, or in some cases going against the current to get to know God better through his Word and prayer?

In this world today, some feel like they are trying to swim against the current called evil.

Do not miss the abundant life God has for you by settling, or worst yet, swimming in the wrong waters.

Prayer Time

God, please give us the desire to get to know you better. This world is full of deceit and empty promises. It is constantly on the move, constantly changing, and some days we feel like we are being swept away by the current everyone else is going down.

Lord, help us to get a grip, to change the direction in our lives if need be, and focus more on you. Help us to invest in you more through prayer and study. It is in those two areas of our lives where we can see the real fruits of our labor. Those things will help give us the foundation we need, the knowledge to build upon.

As Peter prayed, "May grace and peace be lavished on you as you grow in the rich knowledge of God and of Jesus our Lord." Amen.

Yard Sale

One Saturday morning, my daughter and I braved the onslaught of curious onlookers by participating in the community yard sale. I hardly slept thinking about all the questions, the bargaining, the wanting to "make a deal" which would take place that morning as we endeavored to pass along our precious memories, or should I say precious junk. Everyone knows those worn out shoes can fetch fifty cents.

Once word got out about Jesus, and His miracles, and stories, He became the center of attention. He too, would get an onslaught of curious onlookers, and even some not so curious, but more confrontational.

You get confrontational people at a yard sale too.

Look at the following passage:

John 11:45-46: "Then many of the people, who had come with Mary and had seen the things Jesus did, believed in him. But some of them went to the Pharisees and reported to them what Jesus had done."

The crowds followed the signs. They saw, they heard, but still some walked away with nothing. Some walked away in disbelief He would speak such things to them. Some walked away mumbling under their breath the price was too high, how could He expect them to pay that much.

But do you know what the difference is between what Jesus was offering and what I am offering?

What Jesus offered was free to everyone. I was trying to make money at my yard sale, not give stuff away.

What Jesus offers people is still free today.

Prayer Time

Lord, thank you for sending your son to die on the cross for our sins. It is a free gift you offer all of us. It was free to the people then, and it is free to us now.

Everyone loves free things, even at a yard sale Lord, but not everyone is willing to accept your free gift. Bless us today and thank you for your gift. In His name I pray, Amen.

The Cartwheel

When I was a young girl, cartwheels were a lot of fun and something I could do well. We would cart wheel, run, jump, flip and do all kinds of stuff with our bodies as young, potential gymnasts (some in our minds).

A few years ago, I decided to relive my glory days and show off my cart wheeling skills. BIG MISTAKE! My cartwheel was anything but graceful, and I thought I broke both shoulders when I came back up from touching the ground.

Of course, everyone laughed including me -eventually. But what really hit me was I realized I could not do what I used to do, and I should never attempt another cartwheel, back bend, or penny drop - EVER!

Those things happen to all of us at some time or another. We may not be able to do cartwheels anymore, ride horses, work, or do the things we love to do, but it does not mean we can't be used by God to do His work. We can all work for God no matter what stage of life we are in.

Take a look at what it says in Genesis 17:15-17:

"Then God said to Abraham, "As for your wife, you must no longer call her Sarai; Sarah will be her name. I will bless her and will give you a son through her. I will bless her and she will become a mother of nations. Kings of countries will come from her!" Then Abraham bowed down with his face to the ground and laughed as he said to himself, "Can a son be born to a man who is a hundred years old? Can Sarah bear a child at the age of ninety?"

Surely, I am not suggesting you run out and get pregnant.

God was making a covenant with Abraham. He was going to make him a father to the multitude of nations. That must have felt like a big responsibility to Abraham.

The point being - even at a hundred years old, Abraham was still used by God to bring about nations and multitudes of people whom God would be their God, and they would serve Him.

Prayer Time

Lord, may we always remember no matter what stage of life we are in, we can be used for your good purposes to further your kingdom and your righteousness. May we seek direction from you as to how best we can do that. In Jesus' name I pray, Amen.

And all Gods people said?_____

Pebbles

When I was about eleven years old, my good friend and me would toss pebbles into each other's mouths. We would sit about a foot apart, face each other, mouths wide open, both ready to catch rocks. It was like throwing M&M's into each other's mouths, only we were too poor to buy candy, so rocks were the next best thing.

The key to this was you had to trust your friend would throw the pebbles into your mouth and not in your eyes. The other thing we always worried about was chipping a tooth.

I do not know why we never worried about swallowing a pebble should our aim be so exact, but we did not. The more we did it, the better we got. The more we trusted each other, the more rocks we caught. But I have to say there is nothing like the sound of a pebble bouncing off a tooth. It was great fun! Really it was.

It is the same way with God. The more you trust Him, the better it gets. Gods aim is perfect and He never misses. We may move the target around or shut ourselves off, but we can always trust God to do what He says.

Psalms 28:7 says, "The LORD is my strength and my shield; my heart trusts in him, and he helps me. My heart leaps for joy, and with my song, I praise him."

Do you trust God? Do you believe what He says? Does your heart leap for joy? If not, it is never too late to ask Him for help in those areas.

Prayer Time

Father, thank you for caring about us. If we are struggling in the area of trust, may we gather the courage to speak to you about it today. In your son's name I pray, Amen.

Find someone to throw pebbles at. If you are afraid to throw pebbles, try M&Ms, they work just as well. Enjoy! And for goodness sake, close your eyes!

Pebbles Two

Maybe some of you have questions about the pebbles. Maybe you have questions like: Were the pebbles cleaned first? How big were the pebbles used? How do pebbles taste?

To answer your questions: They were dirty, straight from the ground, very small, and tasted gritty. We were not too successful in getting too many into each other's mouth. I think we were more successful in making indentions and scratches on each other's face.

We used to pull our bangs down to protect our foreheads, but it did not help our noses or the rest of our face. Now that I think about it, the teenage acne is not what left holes in my face, it was those little rocks!

When I think about my friend beyond throwing pebbles at me, I think of a trustworthy friend. I could rely on and trust her with my deepest secrets; not sure how deep one can go at eleven and twelve years old. I guess these days, one can go fairly deep.

The definition of trustworthy is "dependable, worthy of being trusted."

Proverbs 11:13 says, "A gossip betrays a confidence, but a trustworthy man keeps a secret."

God is trustworthy and He is the best at keeping secrets. I can tell Him anything and the great thing about having a relationship like that:

1. He is never too busy.

2. He will not gossip.

3. He always has a solution.

4. He loves me unconditionally.

5. I can trust Him with my life.

When you do not think you can trust anyone else, look to the Lord and trust Him. He will gladly be your confidant.

Prayer Time

Father, thank you for your friendship and selfless giving to all who call you Lord. I hope we can always think of you as trust worthy. In Jesus' name I pray all these things, Amen.

I have a question for you. Have you tried it out yet? Have you tried tossing M&M's at each other? I am telling you, it will make you belly laugh like you never have before. And when you are done, you get to eat chocolate!!

Firewood to Idols

How many of you have chopped wood for a fire? Maybe you used it to keep yourself warm. Perhaps you used it to roast marshmallows over a campfire, or roast hot dogs on a skewer.

I was reading Isaiah, Chapter 44 the other day and some particular passages made me laugh aloud. The author was essentially calling someone out, and as funny as it was to me, it got me to thinking about how some in society today do the very same thing. Suddenly, it was not as funny anymore.

Isaiah 44:14-20: "He cuts down cedars, or perhaps took a cypress or an oak. He let it grow among the trees in the forest, or planted a pine, and the rain made it grow. It is mans' fuel for burning, some of it he takes, he warms himself, he kindles fire and bakes bread. But he also fashions a god and worships it; he makes an idol and bows down to it. Half the wood he burns in the fire; over it he prepares his meal, he roasts his meat, and eats his fill. He also warms himself and says "Ah I am warm, I see the fire." From the rest he makes a god, his idol; he bows down and worships it......No one stops to think, no one has the knowledge or understanding to say, "Half of it I used for fuel; I even baked bread over its coal, I roasted meat and I ate. Shall I make a detestable thing from what is left? Shall I bow down to a block of wood?.......Is not this thing in my right hand a lie?"

In summary, this same piece of wood had three uses:

 1) Firewood to keep him warm,

 2) Firewood to cook food and,

3) Wood carved to make an idol to worship.

Isn't it funny how the author is essentially asking "Isn't anyone smart enough to realize what's happening here? Do you not understand what you're doing?"

Tomorrow, we will dive deeper into what the passage is saying. But for now, enjoy a little humor from the Bible and ask yourself this question - Do I have any idols in my life?

Prayer Time

Father, I thank you for today's message. I thank you Lord for the story in Isaiah.

Lord if today, we have any idols in our possession, may we rid them immediately and seek forgiveness. In your son's name I pray, Amen.

Firewood to Idols – continued

Isaiah 44 talks about the many uses for firewood. As we talked previous, you can use a piece of wood to warm yourself, cook food over a fire, or make an idol.

People back in Bible times did that quite frequently. They made idols out of other things as well, not just wood. When Isaiah makes the point about the many uses of a log, it makes you think about what we might make our idols from.

Think about this - What do we make our own gods - money, fame, and power? If we are out to make a god of our own choosing, we deceive ourselves.

Maybe someone should have said something to the people back then like, "You do realize you're worshipping a piece of wood and asking it to provide for you, love you, protect you, and guide you? You just burned half the log over the fire into ashes to be of no more use to you. Now you are worshipping what is left? Really, dude?"

They may have not been familiar with the word, "dude," but you get the idea.

When we think of idols, we think of wood or metal ones.

But Isaiah is really addressing a much deeper issue. He has caused me to ask myself if I have created an idol out of anything or anyone other than God.

Ask yourself these questions as a spot check on idols in your own life.

1. Who created me?

2. Whom do I ultimately trust?

3. Who represents the ultimate truth and where do I look for it?

4. Who can provide me with security and happiness?

5. Who is in charge of my future?

If we are not careful, we may end up serving someone or something else other than God.

No idol ever created anything or anyone. I think we can say with great certainty, no idol ever willingly went to the cross and shed blood for you and me. Amen? Amen! Only one person did that for you and me and His name was Jesus Christ.

Prayer Time

Dear Lord,

Thank you for sending your son to die on the cross for our sin. Thank you for the beautiful trees, which provide so many things. Lord, I know they will never replace you no matter how useful they may be. May we guard our hearts when it comes to idols. In Jesus' name we pray, Amen.

Pin Hole Water Damage

One night I came home to a flooded bathroom and bedroom thanks to a busted pipe in the wall between my kitchen and bathroom. I surveyed the area from where the water might be coming, and low and behold, it was singing from underneath my kitchen sink, behind the wall.

Only the Lord knew how long it had been singing and spewing water. It was seeping out from underneath the baseboards in several areas.

I turned the water off to the house and immediately started soaking up the water. It is not as bad as it sounds. My throw rugs took the hit as well as my bedroom carpet.

I share this with you, not for sympathy or woe is me, but the next morning when I awoke, having not slept well, the only song playing over and over in my head was, "My Jesus, my savior, Lord there is none like you. All of my days, I want to praise, the wonders of your mighty love.... Your my comfort, and my shelter, your my tower of refuge and strength, let every breath, all that I am never cease to worship you.... Shout to the Lord, all the earth let us sing, power and majesty praise to the king, mountains fall down and the seas will roar at the sound of your name.... I sing for joy at the work of your hands, forever I love you, forever, I will stand, nothing compares to the promise I have in you........ Nothing compares to the promise I have in you."

Psalms 59:16-17: "As for me, I will sing about your strength; I will praise your loyal love in the morning; for you are my refuge and my place of shelter when I face trouble. You are my source of strength! I will sing praises to you! For God is my refuge, the God who loves me."

Prayer Time

Father, I am so thankful for the inner peace I have each day. What seemed like an overwhelming event, turned out to be something you so evidently showed you were in control of.

Thank you Father for the way you took care of me. That day was proof once again you were there and you were with me. Father, if anyone is feeling you are far away, will you bring them a "water leak" to let them know you are there.

Well, maybe not a water leak, but you know what I mean Lord. In Jesus' name, Amen.

My First Bike

I have fond memories of my very first bicycle with no training wheels.

It was a rusty, green bike built for a boy. The bar was actually a blessing, because it had no seat, just the pole which welcomes the seat. It was also missing pedals. All it had were bars to receive them.

This fine specimen was the bike I learned to ride on. Difficult? Yes. Impossible? No.

Picture this - As I attempted to ride, I sat on the cross bar, threw my feet underneath the pedal bars and threw them up and around, up and around, and up and around, all the while trying to balance and gain speed.

I wiped out quite a few times, said a few things a seven year old would say, but I kept going back for more. My friends would laugh at me, but eventually, I was riding the bike almost as fast as they could ride.

And the bonus - no one on the block wanted to borrow my bike.

What it taught me though was with very little tools and things not quite the way they should be, I could still do it. We may not have everything we need to get the job done the way we think, but we can use what we have and still succeed. God gives us everything we need, not everything we want. With the things He gives us, we can do great and wonderful things and rest in His power and know He has the rest.

James 1:12 says, "Happy is the one who endures testing, because when he has proven to be genuine, he will receive the crown of life that God promised to those who love him."

My footnote says," the crown of life is like the victory wreath given to winning athletes."

I may not have received a crown for learning how to ride a bike without pedals, but it felt good. But get this - God's crown of life is not glory and honor here on earth, but the reward of eternal life in Heaven with Him- living with God forever!

How do we do that? By loving Him and staying faithful even under pressure.

Prayer Time

Father, I thank you for my rusty, green bicycle. Lord, I can say that now. Lord, it taught me endurance, patience, and some other things. May we look at the rusty, green bicycles in our lives and thank you. In your son's name I pray, Amen.

It is not a Pleasant Memory

The rusty, green bike brought back another bike memory of mine which is not as pleasant. If memory serves me correctly, I was about eight years old at the time.

I had been playing street ball one evening with my friends. Because we did not have a yard big enough, we would play in the streets. I was the pitcher, and I was standing in the middle of the road, pitching the ball to my friends.

On this particular evening, I had pitched the ball, only to turn around and see a guy in his early twenties riding his white, ten-speed bike right at me. I moved out of his way, but he followed.

I started running, and he followed me. I ran from one side of the street to the other, and he followed me. He was purposely chasing me on his bike.

Eventually, I grew tired, and he caught up to me, knocked me down with his front tire, and ran me over in the middle of the street. When I lifted my head, he was already down the road.

I got up and ran to my house, called my big stepbrother. I told him what happened, and he jumped into his car, chased the guy down, and found him. Let's just say I do not think the guy was able to ride his bicycle anymore, at least not for a while.

This story makes me think of what Satan tries with us. He comes after us. He chases us down and tries to wear us out, so eventually we will fall down. And when we fall down, he runs us over, hoping to kill our spirit, hoping we will give in, and give up.

The Bible says Satan prowls around like a roaring lion. Look at what it says in 1 Peter 5:8, "Be sober and alert. Your enemy the devil, *like a roaring lion,* is on the prowl looking for someone to devour."

Satan comes in many forms and fashions, so we have to be alert and stay close to the Lord. If you go onto read verse nine, it talks about resisting and staying strong in your faith.

Prayer Time

Father, may we remain strong in you and resist the enemy. Lord, may we recognize when someone is "chasing us" down. Father, may we draw closer to you more and more every day. In Jesus' name I pray, Amen.

Kids, let this be a lesson to you. Never play ball in the street. I was fortunate it was only a bicycle. It could have been much worse.

Don't go Back There

One night, my friends and I were sitting around in a circle talking as girls do. It was about ten o'clock at night. We were all given permission to stay out late this one night.

Anyway, my middle brother was sitting there with us. As kids usually do, one of my friends dared him to walk through the back alley behind our house - all by himself – the whole length of the alley.

My brother was about eight years old then. Even at eight years old, he was not going to let some girl show him up. He took the challenge.

He was to walk the whole length of the alley, which back then was really long, even to an adult. To get there, he had to walk to the end of the street. He could not cut through someone's yard. So off he went while we waited in anticipation of his return.

About twenty minutes later, we heard blood- curdling screams coming from the same alley behind the houses. They lasted about fifteen seconds or so.

No one moved a muscle. We sat there frightened, staring at each other, looking for some kind of sign one of us would go rescue him.

Of course, everyone looked at me because he was my brother. Sorry bro, I am not going in there. Whoever it was already had one Duby; they were not getting another, and besides none of my friends were in a hurry to go back there and save him. Surely, they would not be in a hurry to save me either.

About three minutes later, what seemed like forever, my brother reappeared. I was so excited to see him, and he was equally excited to see us, and of course, he was displaying his manliness for having taken the dare. I guess he thought we did not hear his girly screams from beyond.

The burning question on everyone's mind - What happened?!?!

Following is his response:

"I was running through the alley way, and ran into barb wired, and it got my legs. Look!"

His pants were ripped slightly, but there was no blood.

It reminded me of a story in the Bible. In Luke 15:3-7, Jesus tells the parable of the lost sheep.

"So Jesus told them this parable: "Which one of you, if he has a hundred sheep and loses one of them, would not leave the ninety-nine in the open pasture and go look for the one which is lost until he finds it? Then when he has found it, he places it on his shoulders, rejoicing. Returning home, he calls together his friends and neighbors, telling them, 'Rejoice with me, because I have found my sheep that was lost.' I tell you, in the same way there will be more joy in heaven over one sinner who repents than over ninety-nine righteous people who have no need to repent."

Stay tuned tomorrow for, as Paul Harvey used to say, "the rest of the story." In the meantime, let us pray.

Prayer Time

Father I want to thank you for the good shepherd, your son, Jesus. He was wonderful at telling parables to make it easy for us to understand the real message. Thanks for your love and I pray for wisdom. To you be all the honor and glory, Amen.

I Told You Not to Go Back There

I told the story about my brother going into the dark alley, and screaming when he ran into the barbwire. As mentioned, it reminded me of the parable Jesus told in Luke 15. You might be asking "What's the correlation here?"

Pretend for a moment, you are a sheep. You can be a big fluffy sheep or a skinny sheep. I'll let you choose.

As a sheep, you are grazing with ninety-nine other sheep in a beautiful, green pasture. Some you know, some you do not know. I will let you pick that also.

Everything is going well. The sky is beautiful, the weather balmy, and you have plenty of wide-open space in which to graze. However, you have a sheep friend who decides they are going to wander off by themselves and be a loner sheep, and off they go. We all have sheep like that in our immediate circle. At least I do.

The shepherd notices a sheep is missing. After all, he counts sheep, not to help himself go to sleep at night, but because he cares for and has a responsibility to make sure all sheep have been accounted for. He goes in search of your sheep friend. He finds him and brings him back to the herd. Then he celebrates over finding the loner sheep. You may or may not celebrate the loner sheep coming back, but God does.

God loves it when a sinner repents. Guess what? I am a sinner from way back and God loves it when I repent.

You know, when my brother wandered off and took the dare, he got himself into trouble back there in the alley. He could have been hurt very badly. The sheep in the parable who wandered off could have been hurt badly too had the shepherd not found it.

My point is when we really mess up, get full of ourselves, or make a bad or unwise decision, we can get ourselves into trouble and think we cannot come back, or no one cares, but God does. He is like the shepherd who went looking for the lost sheep and rejoiced. God rejoices over our repentance. He sent us a shepherd in Jesus Christ who as He says, "lays down his life for his sheep."

Do you know the shepherd?

Prayer Time

Father, I am thankful I have a shepherd who is willing to lay down his life for me. Thank you for giving me life, and for your mercy and grace. Your love is unending, never failing. Some days I act like a sheep and start to wander away. Thank you for rescuing me. In your son's name I pray, Amen.

If you do not know this shepherd, we can help you. Go to my website and find out how. The web address is on the back of this book.

When We Wander Away

Now that you have pretended to be a sheep, lets' talk about what can happen when you really do wander away from the herd.

What happens when a sheep wanders off alone?

Who or what is out there prowling around?

What trouble could a lonely sheep get into?

Is the grass really greener on the other side?

When sheep stay in the big group, there's protection. Two things protect them- one being the group itself, and the other being the shepherd.

When a sheep is in the big group, he has company, he is taken care of. He does not have to worry as much about predators. He or she can do sheep things like stand around, graze on grass or sleep. But when the sheep wanders away, suddenly all those things are left behind.

Remember when I shared about my brother being bit by the barb wire? Sheep can be bit as well, and sometimes they can be devoured.

When we wander away from the protection of our Heavenly Father, we flirt with danger. Like sheep, we can be led astray. Like sheep, we can fall over the cliff. Our legs can be chewed on, or even worse, the enemy can devour us. Yuck!

The enemy entices us, and he longs to lead us away from our Heavenly Father.

Have you ever wondered why Satan does not go after lost people? They are already lost. What is the point? His aim is believers, people who believe in Jesus Christ as their Lord and Savior. If he can lead them away, keep them busy doing non-kingdom things, tempt them or even worse, devour them, then he is succeeding. He is winning the battle in people's lives.

Who will you choose this day?

Prayer Time

Father, help us stay close to you. Lord, may your hedge of protection always surround us and keep us safe. Father, the grass may look greener on the other side, but Father you know it leads to a dead end.

Lord my prayer is if we know anyone who has wandered away from the herd, Lord we pray they come back quickly. Lord, if we know people who have never been part of the herd, who do not know Jesus as their personal Lord and Savior, God we pray for them too. In your son's name, I pray all these things, Amen.

Do you know some sheep who have wandered away from the herd? Pray for them today. Reach out to them today before it is too late!

The shepherd is waiting......

Plug into the Power

I have a very healthy respect for electricity. Electricity earned my respect when I was twelve years old. One night I went to plug my bedroom lamp in, not knowing the back of the plug had fallen off. My finger mistakenly took the place of the plastic cover, and upon making connection with 120 amps, my bottom found a new seat across the bedroom.

I mention this because when we plug into Jesus there's a change, but it's not hurtful. There's an excitement, a charge if you will when we plug into His power.

The author of "Life's Healing Choices" tells us that we need to plug into Gods' power. It's like plugging a toaster into the wall. If we don't plug the toaster in, our bread isn't going to toast. We need the electricity. If we don't pay the bill, there's no power.

If we don't plug into Gods power, we won't be able to enjoy the fullness of what He has for us.

Like the defective plug that sent me flying across the room, we're defective, yet we can plug into the power, God's power, and enjoy an exciting and fulfilling life.

Plug in!

Prayer Time

Father, thank you for the ability to be able to plug into your power. Thank you for the opportunity we have to enjoy a relationship with you. It's exciting and thrilling all in one, much like being plugged into 120 amps, well, if I was a toaster. You know what I mean Father. I love you and I am so thankful I can call you daddy. In Jesus' name I pray, Amen.

Do the Math

4x / 3c +25b (x of 7) - pie r squared = X.

You may know the answer to that math problem, but I sure don't. I never made it past Geometry in the tenth grade, and Algebra in the ninth grade was a horrific experience for me. So much so, it was the first time I ever received an "F" in school and the last. I had always worked hard to get good grades. Not just good, but great.

My friend, allow me to share another equation that I do know the answer to - *now*. It took me many years to figure this one out, but now that I know the answer, I want to share it with everyone I meet.

Please insert your name in the equation below.

_____ + God = A fulfilled life

_____ + God = A life like no other

_____ + faith = God filled life

_____ + Jesus = Relationship

_____ + God = Salvation, forgiveness, redemption, joy, happiness.

You see, God must be part of the equation. Not only is He part of the equation, but He is also part of the answer, if not *THE* answer. To leave God out of the equation is like leaving milk out of cereal, bees out of honey, green out of grass, fiber out of whole grain. It simply doesn't work. We can try to make a go at it without God, but I don't believe we will experience the completeness in our lives that only God can produce.

God must be part of our life equation.

Next, we'll take a look at what an equation looks like without God in it. I think you'll be surprised at the results.

Prayer Time

Father thank you for this simple lesson you gave me the other day. You must be part of the equation for us to really get it. May we be purposeful in our daily calculations. In Jesus' name I pray, amen.

Do the Math Part 2

Previously, I talked about Math. I suggested that God must be part of the equation. I still believe that today.

What happens when He isn't part of the equation? What happens when we leave Him out?

What kind of equations do we get when we leave God out of our lives?

Without Jesus in our hearts and having accepted Him as our Lord and Savior, our equations might look something like this:

Feel free to insert your name on the line.

_____ + pride = Fall

_____ + unforgiveness = Bitterness

_____ + unhealthy fear = Doubt

_____ + worldly possessions = Emptiness

_____ + no love = Loneliness

_____ + without Jesus = Lost

The last equation is the most devastating one, because us without Jesus leads to all of the above equations. When I look at those, I really don't see any real joy or happiness. Do you?

What's your equation look like? Is God part of the equation in your life?

Listen folks, and this is a good one to share with your friends - it's not too late to sharpen your Math skills.

It's not too late to correct some of the answers. It's not too late to make God a permanent part of the equation.

Do it today, don't delay.

I was a poet and didn't know it!

Sorry. Now I'm crossing over to literature. I better go for now while this can still be saved.

Prayer Time

Father thank you for being part of my equation - for being the answer I had been looking for all those years. In Jesus' name I pray, Amen.

Tutoring = Discipling

While I'm on the subject of Math, it reminded me of tutors.

Tutors have an important role in the lives of children. They help children with various tasks like Math, Reading, and other subjects that may be challenging. Their assistance may last a few days, a few weeks, or a few months.

Christians should think of themselves as tutors. When a man, woman, or child accepts Jesus into their heart for the first time, Christians should disciple them. If you don't know what disciple means, think of tutoring. We should be walking alongside them, teaching, mentoring, guiding, sharing our faith, and reading the Bible together.

If we simply baptize and send them on their way, to flounder about, we have not done our job of disciplining or tutoring them. We told them where they need to go without giving them the directions. We told them what they need to do, and who they need, without telling them how - we've given them no explanation.

There's a real possibility that new believers will get frustrated and walk away never fully experiencing all that God has for them. There are those who will exhibit determination and seek out the answers. They will dig deeper and attempt to get at the core of their new found faith. Sadly, all too often, a lot of new believers struggle and fall back. It's as if they walked through the front door of the church only to walk out the back door soon after their new found faith.

The idea behind discipling people is so those people can disciple others. If we don't do a good job discipling new believers, those new believers won't be able to disciple others. They won't get to experience all God has for them, and neither will many others.

If someone had not taken the time to disciple me, I wouldn't be where I am today. I would have missed out on everything that has happened in my life over the last fourteen years. Those who have invested in me, thank you for taking the time. May God richly bless you for your sacrifice. I thank my heavenly Father for you and to Him be the glory! Amen!

Rejecting God

Let's check out 1 Samuel 8:1-18:

"In his old age Samuel appointed his sons as judges over
Israel. The name of his firstborn son was Joel, and the
name of his second son was Abijah. They were judges in
Beer Sheba. But his sons did not follow his ways. Instead,
they made money dishonestly, accepted bribes, and
perverted justice. So all the elders of Israel gathered
together and approached Samuel at Ramah. They said to
him, "Look, you are old, and your sons don't follow your
ways. So now appoint over us a king to lead us, just like
all the other nations have." But this request displeased
Samuel, for they said, "Give us a king to lead us." So
Samuel prayed to the Lord. The Lord said to Samuel, "Do
everything the people request of you. For it is not you
that they have rejected, but it is me that they have
rejected as their king. Just as they have done from the
day that I brought them up from Egypt until this very
day, they have rejected me and have served other gods.
This is what they are also doing to you. So now do as
they say. But seriously warn them and make them aware
of the policies of the king who will rule over them." So
Samuel spoke all the words of the Lord to the people
who were asking him for a king. He said, "Here are the
policies of the king who will rule over you: He will
conscript your sons and put them in his chariot forces
and in his cavalry; they will run in front of his chariot. He
will appoint for himself leaders of thousands and leaders
of fifties, as well as those who plow his ground, reap his

harvest, and make his weapons of war and his chariot equipment. He will take your daughters to be ointment makers, cooks, and bakers. He will take your best fields and vineyards and give them to his own servants. He will demand a tenth of your seed and of the produce of your vineyards and give it to his administrators and his servants. He will take your male and female servants, as well as your best cattle and your donkeys, and assign them for his own use. He will demand a tenth of your flocks, and you yourselves will be his servants. In that day you will cry out because of your king whom you have chosen for yourselves, but the Lord won't answer you in that day."

There are a few points I'd like to highlight here from the lesson I just studied that I thought were interesting:

1. The people were ultimately rejecting God by insisting on a king.

2. This new king would take from them their first fruits, he would demand a tenth. Ultimately he will take from them what should be given to God first.

3. He will enslave them.

4. The people will serve other gods as some have always done.

5. He will take from the people and give to whom he chooses.

6. The people will cry out to God but he will not hear them.

Allow me to ask you a question - Whom do we serve, God or man?

If we serve man, we make a grave mistake. If we choose to cry out for a king to lead us instead of God almighty, we've made a wrong turn down a road that will lead to destruction.

Prayer Time

Lord I pray we haven't made the wrong turn already, but there are days God, where it sure feels like we have. If we're headed down the wrong road, may we recognize our mistake, turn to you, repent, and make the path straight. You are whom we should serve; not man, not money, not power, nor influence. Father, please forgive us our sins and cleanse us anew. In Jesus' name I pray, Amen.

Bad Hair Cut

I have never been one to be adventurous when it comes to cutting my own hair. But foregoing my fears, I decided to give it a shot. After all, saving money these days is something I'm attempting to do (not too well I might add, but trying).

I had watched numerous people cut my hair in years past. Each had their own way, but they all ended with the same result - what I considered to be a good haircut, one that was even, stylish, and professional looking.

So with guts a plenty and scissors ready, I began the work of cutting my own hair. This turned into a two day process. A snip here, a snip there, a not so good snip there and a correction snip there. Let's just say, there were more correction snips and cuts then there were good cuts. I realized I could not do the job my predecessors had done.

To further confirm my misgivings about the job I had done, a dear friend of mine whom would have been the last person I thought to ever notice, asked me who cut my hair and commented "they really did a poor job, I mean, don't you think?"

I knew I was in trouble if he had noticed a bad haircut. What must everyone else be thinking and with that, I went to a professional place right away and gave the stylist plenty of laughter as she tried to fix my butcher job. Thankfully, most of the butchering was done on the under layers and not readily on the top.

Needless to say, I learned a very important lesson - save my money for haircuts *always* - never attempt it on my own!

It's the same with God. So often times, we attempt things on our own, things we know very well we should leave to God, and God alone. But I know for me, I get so excited about something, I get inpatient, I get brave about something, and I run full steam ahead of Him, only to discover I made a grievous error back at the decision making - the time I should have let God handle it, and *go before me*. I would have saved myself a lot of bad hair days!

Psalm 25:4, "Show me your ways, O Lord, teach me your paths; guide me in your truth and teach me, for you are God my savior."

In Jesus' name I thank you Lord, Amen.

Lonely Orange Tree

One day I was out in the back yard working on a few things, and I took notice of my lonely orange tree. I had given up on that orange tree last year. It had taken a few beatings from the cooler weather in the past few years, and looked like it was on its way out. Being anything but a fruitologist, I gave up on the tree and accepted defeat. I'm not sure "fruitologist" is a real word, but I needed something descriptive for my lack of skill with anything green. This is no reflection on people with real skills to grow fruit trees.

I had let it go so badly that what I called a weed (the lawn man said, "a natural bush for this area") had taken root, entwined itself, and had almost overtaken my orange tree completely. But as I approached the orange tree, I saw among the "very tall weeds" an orange. There it was, a pretty round fruit hanging from the branch. I pulled the weeds to the side and there were a few more. I couldn't believe it! My tree had actually survived the bitter winter, and somehow managed to gain strength and produce fruit.

Sometimes we go through trials in our lives that attempt to choke the life out of us, or prevent us from producing fruit. When it seems like all hope is lost, and you're ready to give into the choking weeds around you, break forth, and reach towards the sunlight; reach towards the Savior, Jesus Christ. Accept His strength, take hold of his hand and don't let go. You have a purpose here on this earth and it's not to be choked out by any weeds.

Prayer Time

Father, this morning I come to you and thank you for showing me that no matter what we go through in this life, we should never give up hope in you. We should put our trust and faith in you, and know that even for a season, we may get choked out by the weeds that try and overtake us. But somewhere in the midst, we are reaching forth to grab your hand, and be saved from the muck and the mire, from the things that try and bind us up. Thanks daddy, I love you. In Jesus' name I pray, Amen.

I am so grateful for you!

Lonely Orange Tree - Part 2

My orange tree had been surrounded and almost overtaken by what I called a weed with pretty little flowers. You could no longer see the ground, or the trunk of the tree. The weed had practically blanketed it with its vines. The branches above were covered in this weed. It's when I pulled the weed to the side, that the fruit was revealed.

I started pulling the weed from the tree, and as I grabbed parts of it, its vines pricked my hands. Not only had it overtaken my orange tree, but it had developed prickly barbs along its vine. The only way to remove it was to use gloves and some cutters. The good news is that the weed could be removed from the orange tree with a little work and determination. The orange tree could show off its beautiful fruit once again. It could fully soak in the sunshine. It could continue to thrive and not be choked out by the weed.

We can do that too my friend. Who is your gardener? Who can remove the weeds in your life that long to choke the life out of you?

Jesus Christ that's who. Jesus Christ can remove the weeds in our lives that long to choke the life out of us; that long to overtake us.

As I think about removing those weeds from my orange tree, the branches and leaves on the tree would have to move and bend from the force of me pulling the weeds away. We too will have to move and bend as Jesus works on us.

John 15:1-2 says this, "I am the true vine, and my Father is the gardener. He cuts off every branch in me that bears no fruit, while every branch that bears fruit he prunes so that it will be even more fruitful."

Prayer Time

Lord, thank you for being the gardener in our lives. Father, strengthen us to go through the process of ridding the weeds that long to choke the life out of us. May we continue to reach toward your hand, to draw closer to you each and every day. In Jesus' name I pray and am thankful for, Amen.

"Marco Polo"

As a child, I remember playing numerous games of Marco Polo in my grandmother's swimming pool. If you have never played this game before (I guess you wouldn't if you never had a pool), the game is for everyone in the pool. One person closes their eyes and yells "Marco," while the others respond with "Polo." The person playing Marco is to find the Polo's and tag them while their eyes are closed. The Polo's can go under water to move around, but they are not supposed to get out of the pool *brother!!!* Can you tell my brother usually cheated by getting out of the pool, and running to the other end to escape being tagged?

Whoever the Marco tags, that person becomes the new Marco and the game continues. It is a lot of fun.

When I thought of this memory, it reminded me of something important I wanted to share with you. Jesus is not hiding from us or the world. He is not playing Marco Polo with us. However, there are some people who *are* playing this game with Jesus. There are some people playing Marco and there are some playing Polo. Those people have their reasons for playing this game with Jesus. What those reasons are, I do not know. Maybe they are playing it out of fear, perhaps it's out of shame. There's a real possibility they don't know Jesus at all. Maybe they heard about Him in church or on the TV. Maybe they simply wish to hide from Him and pretend He doesn't exist at all.

The question for us today - Are you playing Marco Polo with Jesus?

Prayer Time

Father, this morning, we come to you for comfort, wisdom, and direction. Are we playing the game of Marco Polo with your son, Jesus Christ? If we are Lord, may we come out of the shadows and take His hand. If we are ashamed of something, may we seek His face and make it right. You sent your son, Jesus Christ, into this world to save us from our sin, to be the atoning sacrifice for us all. May we remember the real reason he came to this earth. In Jesus' name I pray, Amen.

Those Old Trophies

A few months ago, I was rummaging through the garage cleaning some things out when I stumbled across an unfamiliar box. It's one of those boxes you tuck away, because you'll need whatever's inside it someday.

I opened the box, and to my surprise were all my old trophies from school. Wrapped in newspaper, were my trophies for Archery, Volleyball, Softball, Bowling, Best Poached Eggs (yes, Best Poached Eggs in the Southeast), and Lioness of the Year. I was quite the sports woman in my day. Now I am fortunate if I can actually jog down the street. Here they were all wrapped up in a box, stowed away for remembrance sake.

Do you remember the excitement you felt when you received Jesus into your heart? Do you remember how wonderful it was to receive that gift, the gift of the Savior who came into this world to die on the cross and forgive your sins? More so, what have you done with the gift of life?
Have you stowed it away in a lonely box like old trophies to one day be stumbled upon and remembered? Are you displaying your love for Jesus like a trophy on a shelf? Are you growing closer to Jesus Christ every day? Is Jesus Christ just a trophy to you? "I got him, now let's move onto the next trophy?"
What's your trophy box look like?

Listen, we can have all the trophies in the world. We can have the mirror ball trophy from the television show. We can have the super bowl rings and other fancy things, but if we don't have Jesus Christ as our Lord and Savior, all those trophies and trinkets mean NOTHING!

Got Jesus? Here's a familiar passage from scripture we need reminding of - John 3:16-17:

"For God so loved the world that he gave his one and only son, that whoever believes in him shall not perish but have eternal life." For God did not send his Son into the world to condemn the world, but to save the world through Him."

Prayer Time

Thank you Father for the gift of your son, Jesus Christ. May we do more with Him then display Him as a trophy we have collected in our life. In Jesus' name I pray, Amen.

How to Pray

People often wonder how they should pray. They ask questions like:

Should I close my eyes?

Should I fold my hands?

Should I get down on one knee or stand on one foot?

Are there certain words I should say to guarantee God would hear my prayers?

These are all very good questions to ask. But can I share something with you? I do not believe there is a magic formula or set of motions we have to exercise to pray.

I believe God hears our prayers whether we are driving in a car, on our knees, walking along or sitting in a church pew.

Did you know Jesus gave us a model prayer as an example? You bet!

In Matthew, Chapter 6, Jesus teaches the disciples and us about prayer. It is often known as the Lords' Prayer because Jesus gave it to us as a model to keep in mind as we pray.

It is very easy to be caught up in the "I want I want, I need, I need, and I must have these things" type prayers. Sometimes we get so busy with the, "I want and I need," we forget to thank God for what we have already received. We forget to praise Him and His majesty. We forget to ask for His forgiveness.

Jesus gave us a model which can be duplicated many times over. We can praise God and thank Him for His provisions. We can honor His name. We can ask for His will to be done. We can ask Him for help with our daily struggles and so much more.

Consistent prayer life can lead to a beautiful relationship with the creator, our Heavenly Father. It is not wrong to come to God with the same concerns every time. Where we go astray is when we speak empty words just to hear ourselves speak.

Jesus says in Matthew 6:9-13:

"This, then, is how you should pray: "Our Father in heaven, hallowed be thy name, your kingdom come, your will be done on earth as it is in heaven. Give us today our daily bread. Forgive us our debts, as we also have forgiven our debtors. And lead us not into temptation, but deliver us from the evil one."

We tend to want to make our prayers fancy and formal, but may I suggest something to you?

Start talking to God today, and talk to Him as if you were talking to your best friend about some hot shoes you just saw at the mall. Maybe you just saw a hotrod driving down the street. Just start talking to Him, and you will be surprised at what you experience. Just be sure you thank Him and praise Him for what He has already done in your life.

Your prayer life will change and it will deepen as time goes by.

Need a Speaker for a Women's Event or Dinner?

Are you looking for something to excite your group?

Perhaps you need motivation or a refreshing way to connect with God in this fast-paced world we live in.

Have you fallen into a spiritual groove?

I am a forty six year old single mom who works full time, recently graduated college, teaches classes, and is in love with the Lord.

Are you asking yourself right now, "How can she do all that and still be able to come and share with us?"

Let me help you get up and get moving. Let me help you get excited for the Lord again. I would love to share with you and your group ways to get moving and reconnect to the Lord through sharing some laughs, some heartache, and some real heartfelt inspiration about God, His love, and His passion.

We will laugh, we will cry, we will get real.

Would You Like More Information?

Visit our website at http://www.thefruitwars.com

What is on the site?

    -New Blog Posts

    -Resources

    -Who Is Jesus?

    -What we Believe

    -Helpful Links and Books

Follow us on Twitter: @thefruitwars

Like our Facebook Page: The Fruit Wars

Email: thefruitwars@gmail.com

Bibliography

*-Life Application Study Bible - NIV version –
Tyndale House Publishers Inc. Carole Stream, IL
and Zondervan, Grand Rapids, Michigan*

-Bible.org

-My Memories

-Jeff Dixon - Foreword

NOTES

NOTES

Proof

Made in the USA
Charleston, SC
14 May 2013